Incontri in Italia

Italia, le regioni

Incontri in Italia

A BBC radio course

Italian text and notes by
Giovanni Carsaniga, Dott. Lett. (Pisa)
Lecturer in Italian at the University of Sussex
and
Anna-Laura Lepschy, B.Litt., M.A. (Oxon)
Lecturer in Italian at University College, London

Produced by Elsie Ferguson and Ann Caldwell

First broadcast on Radio 3 (Study) in 1968
Rebroadcast twice in 1971:
on Radio 4 at 10.30 a.m. on Saturdays starting 19 June
and
on Radio 3 (Study) at 6.30 p.m. on Tuesdays starting 22 June
(for full details see *Radio Times*)

British Broadcasting Corporation

Pianta d'Italia con le località nominate nel testo

Contents

Introduction

This course of fifteen lessons is intended for those of you who already know some Italian and are interested in Italy and its civilization. It is not meant to teach you a few phrases to be learned by heart and repeated in a holiday situation, but to give you an insight into the general structure of Italian sentences, so that you can use even a limited vocabulary correctly and flexibly.

Many of us have learnt foreign languages largely through reading and writing, not only because of the way we have been taught at school, but also because, though it sounds different, a foreign word often looks like its equivalent in English. Your ability to understand what is written (which is greater than you imagine) may not mean that you can understand and reproduce the right foreign sounds. Indeed what is commonly called 'reading knowledge' of a language seldom does. This is why we want you to listen and speak, as well as to read.

Since broadcasting time is precious, we shall not be giving you instructions and explanations during the broadcast; they are to be found in this book. We want you to treat it as an integral part of the course, and to study each lesson before the broadcast.

GRAMMAR

In the notes we have tried to keep the number of grammatical terms down to the very minimum. We have, however, found it necessary to use a few basic terms which we will now explain in case you are not familiar with them.

Italian is a strongly **inflected** language, that is to say the way the sentence is constructed is shown not only by the order of its words but also by their endings.

When speaking, we need to know and to make known the following:

a The **person.** This is made clear in English mostly by the use of pronouns – **I** walked, **he** walked etc. In Italian it is usually shown by changing the endings of the verbs – *camminavo*, *camminava* etc. This is why personal pronouns are used much less often in Italian than in English.

b The time referred to, the **tense** (from an old word meaning 'time').

c The **number** (humans, animals, or things). The only distinction relevant to grammar is between one – **singular** – and more than one – **plural**.

d The type or kind of the person or persons – the **gender** (from an old word meaning 'kind'). In English gender corresponds to a distinction between the sexes of people or animals. In Italian all words naming things must belong either to the **masculine** or the **feminine** gender.

Person, tense, number and gender combine in Italian in two main inflexion systems: [1] Person-Tense-Number and [2] Gender-Number.

Words inflected in the Person-Tense-Number system are called **verbs.** Verb-inflexion, or **conjugation**, may appear complicated at first sight, because of the large number of verb endings. In fact they follow reasonably regular patterns: e.g. the 1st person plural always ends in *-mo* and the 2nd plural always in *-te*.

Words inflected in the Gender-Number system are either **nouns** or **adjectives**. Nouns are words that, in both Italian and English, may be accompanied by an article. Adjectives are not accompanied by an article. There are two basic patterns in Italian into which most nouns and adjectives fall:

Pattern 1

	sing.	plur.
m.	-o	-i
f.	-a	-e

Pattern 2

	sing.	plur.
m./f.	-e	-i

gatto (*cat*)   nero (*black*)
gatto nero   gatti neri
gatta nera   gatte nere

tigre (*tiger*)   crudele (*cruel*)
tigre crudele   tigri crudeli

There are, however, a few other patterns, two of which we shall meet during this course. The ending of the word is not necessarily a sufficient clue to its gender and number. These often need to be confirmed by the **article**. Here is a reminder of the two types of article:

	DEFINITE			INDEFINITE		
	1	2	3	1	2	3
m. sing.	il	lo	l'	un	uno	un
m. plur.	i	gli				
f. sing.	la		l'	una		un'
f. plur.	le					

1 followed by words beginning with a consonant

2 followed by s + consonant, gn-, z- or ps-

3 followed by initial vowel

Make a point of learning all new words together with their appropriate articles.

A qualifying adjective must always have the same gender and number as the noun it qualifies. Verbs and their subjects must have the same number and person. This is what is called **agreement**. Agreement does not necessarily mean that agreeing nouns and adjectives must have the same ending, since the noun may belong to Pattern 1 and the adjective to Pattern 2 or vice versa.

Many words do not belong to either inflexion system, and are therefore invariable, such as **adverbs**, **conjunctions** and **prepositions**.

It is essential to realize that the above definitions do not apply to what the words sound or look like, but to what they *do* in a sentence. Take, for instance, the English word 'plane': it may be a noun, 'flat surface', a verb, 'to smooth down', an adjective, 'two-dimensional'. Likewise the Italian *piano* may be a noun, *il piano della tavola* – 'the surface of the table', an adjective, *un terreno piano* – 'a flat piece of ground', an adverb, *parlava piano* – 'he or she spoke softly'.

As we said at the beginning, the number of words you should be able to recognize is much larger than the number you can actively recollect. In fact, if you are observant, you can probably guess, in their context, the meaning of hundreds of words you have never seen before. You have no doubt met the Italian word *stazione* – 'station'. Perhaps you also know that *nazione* means 'nation'. You may, therefore, realize that many (though not all) Italian words ending in *-zione* correspond very closely to English words ending in -tion: *azione* – 'action', *federazione* – 'federation', *nozione* – 'notion' etc. You may also notice that all such words are feminine. We will point out to you a few more analogies of this type, which will help you to build up quite a large and useful vocabulary.

You must, however, bear in mind that the exact meaning of a word is controlled by the context in which it appears, that is, by the other words in the sentence. This is why it is so important that you should learn, not lists of words, but how to form sentences correctly. Vocabulary and grammar are skills that must be developed together. And finally, remember that the **meaning** of an Italian word or phrase should **not** be identified with its English **translation** e.g. the verb *piacere* is nearly always translated as 'to like': *mi piace il vino* – 'I like wine'; but what it actually means in Italian is 'to please' – 'wine pleases me'.

PRONUNCIATION

Pronunciation cannot be taught by a book. Make a point of listening carefully and imitating the speakers to the best of your ability. Bear in mind that the better your own pronunciation, the better you will understand others when they speak Italian. And good pronunciation will also help you to read and write correctly, since it is only by steady practice in associating spoken sounds with their written form that you will learn to recognize what you read.
The following points are important:

1 Italian spelling is more 'phonetic' than English: by and large, each letter of the alphabet, or each group of letters, such as -ch-, -gh-, -gn-, -gl-, represent one sound only; unlike English, where, for instance -ough represents six different sounds: bough, cough, though, through, tough, and borough.

2 Whatever their position in the word, vowel sounds must be uttered clearly with no 'glides'. *Roma*, for instance, should not be pronounced as 'roamer', or *uso* as 'you so'. Bearing in mind what we have said about inflexion, you will realize that the clear pronunciation of endings (nearly all Italian words end in a vowel) is particularly important.

3 Certain initial consonants in English, such as p- in pin and t- in tea, are **aspirated**, that is, their pronunciation is accompanied by an audible puff of breath through the lips (try saying 'pin' with your fingertips just before your lips; you will feel it). No Italian initial consonant is aspirated: therefore in saying words like *pino* – 'pine tree' and *testa* – 'head', try to reduce as far as possible the emission of air through your lips.

4 The pronunciation of double consonants is also very important, since the meaning of a number of words depends on it: *pala* – 'shovel', *palla* – 'ball'. When pronouncing double consonants, as well as strengthening the sound of the consonant itself, you should also shorten the length of the preceding vowel.

5 In Italian, as in English, there are pairs of words of identical spelling, whose meaning is distinguished only by a different stress (think of re**c**ord and re**c**ord). It is, therefore, essential that you should learn the correct position for the stress on every word e.g. *papa* and *papà*, *ancora* and *ancora*.

6 When speaking, you should not think of individual words but of phrases containing several words strung together. In speech, unlike writing, there are no empty gaps between one word and the next. Pay special attention to the way in which the speaker's voice rises and falls. This is called **intonation**, and a good intonation is just as important as a good accent. The ability to recognize the different patterns of intonation can help you to understand the meaning of what you hear: for example, in Italian a question often has the same form as a statement, the only difference being in the intonation. G.C.

1 Milano

Milano, ingresso della Galleria in piazza del Duomo

Milan is the industrial and commercial centre of Italy. Every year seventy thousand southern workers arrive to find work and to make money, a part of which they will send to their relatives left behind in the poor areas of the South, perhaps in Calabria, where soil, climate and lack of raw materials for industry all conspire to make life a day to day struggle against poverty.

These workers who emigrate to the North, find a different way of life, different people speaking a different dialect, another language almost, and they find a city whose skyline has been transformed in recent years by skyscraper buildings and tall blocks of offices and flats. They find too that the pace of life tends to be faster and that people walk with a more purposeful air.

Within the city are the commercial offices, banks and shops; the Via Monte Napoleone has some of the finest and most expensive shops and boutiques in Italy. The factories are outside the city, in a great belt of modern development which has swallowed up the little villages and some of the fertile agricultural lands of the rich Lombardy plain. Milan and the surrounding areas have a great diversity of industry, engineering being particularly important. The manufacture of textiles, and silk, for which mulberries were planted in the Lombardy plain centuries ago, supplies the fashion industry in which Italy, a very fashion conscious country, plays a leading role.

In spite of modern development, however, Milan's most famous building remains the cathedral. The great square in which it stands, the Piazza del Duomo, has modern shops, offices, banks and restaurants, and a sign indicating the Underground, but the cathedral itself is almost six hundred years old. It was built by Gian Galeazzo Visconti, Duke of Milan, as an offering to the Virgin in return for a son and heir. He was an ambitious man, and dreamed of becoming king of Italy, hoping that he would be crowned in his great cathedral which, when projected, was to be the largest church in existence. In size it is now superseded by St. Peter's in Rome, but it remains nevertheless one of the most ornate Gothic cathedrals ever built. The exterior is adorned with thousands of pinnacles and statues, so numerous that few people have been tempted to count them. On top is the golden, floodlit Madonna, called *La Madonnina* by the people of Milan.

Work on the cathedral continued over the centuries, until the present one when the great bronze doors were added. When a job or a piece of work seems to be taking a long time, the Milanese say: *È come la fabbrica del duomo* – 'it's like the building of the cathedral'.

Not far from the cathedral is the Scala Opera House, built on the site of a church: Santa Maria della Scala, which had become derelict. The opening night of the Opera season traditionally takes place on the 8th December, the day set aside by the Milanese to honour their patron saint, Sant'Ambrogio, who was bishop of Milan in the earliest days of Christianity, and who, it is said, introduced hymn singing into churches. The Milanese are sometimes called Ambrosiani after their saint.

Italians say that it is either too hot or too cold in Milan. Winters are cold and often foggy, and in summer there is a heavy, humid heat. Fortunately the lakes and mountains are only a short drive away. A small plane operates between Milan and Cortina d'Ampezzo flying between the peaks of the Dolomites rather than above them, and this is probably the best way to see this very beautiful mountain range. Motorways (*autostrade*), link Milan with most of the main towns of Italy.

Rice is eaten in the north of Italy as an alternative to *pasta*, and *risotto alla milanese* is one of the special dishes of Milan. This is rice cooked in butter and chicken broth and flavoured with saffron. As a general rule rice is not served with meat in Italy, but is often cooked with meat, fish or vegetables as flavouring. *Risotto alla milanese* is, however, traditionally served as an accompaniment to another of Milan's special dishes: *osso buco*, which is shin of veal stewed in wine, stock and tomatoes and topped with chopped parsley, a little garlic and some grated lemon peel.

Programmi per le vacanze

Siamo nella mensa della Ditta Felice Cossogno & Figli, una piccola fabbrica in una cittadina vicino a Milano. Questa fabbrica produce motori elettrici per lavatrici, frigoriferi ed altri elettrodomestici.

Sono quasi le due del pomeriggio. L'ingegner Mario Garbiati, direttore tecnico, il dottor Giovanni Giudice, vice-direttore dell'ufficio commerciale, e la signorina Luisa Marzullo, la sua segretaria, bevono il caffè e conversano.

MARIO GARBIATI Gio', vuoi aprire la finestra vicino a te per favore? Comincia a far caldo.

GIOVANNI GIUDICE Ma certo! Ecco fatto!

LUISA MARZULLO Che tempo magnifico! E noi invece dovremo star chiusi in ufficio tutto il pomeriggio!

M. Andiamo, signorina! Via . . . Perchè non pensa alle prossime vacanze . . . Il pomeriggio è noioso? Allora immagini di non essere in ufficio, cominci a fantasticare, a far programmi per l'estate . . .

G. Bravo! che razza di consigli che dai alla mia segretaria. Mentre lei fa castelli in aria, e immagina di non essere in ufficio, come dici tu, chi sbrigherà tutta la corrispondenza arretrata?

L. Non stia in pensiero, dottore. Niente fantasie: i miei piani son già bell'e fatti. Andrò per un mesetto in Puglia, dai nonni. È da qualche anno che non ci vado, e loro vogliono assolutamente vedermi quest'estate.

M. Già deciso? Beata Lei che non ha problemi! Invece, a casa mia . . . mia figlia vuole andare al mare . . .

G. . . . e tua moglie, scommetto, in montagna.

M. E io non so che pesci pigliare!

L. E suo figlio?

M. Ah, lui non mi dà troppo fastidio. Farà un viaggio per conto suo, chissà dove. Sa come sono oggi i ragazzi! Amano l'indipendenza, niente famiglia tra i piedi . . .

L. Allora, come risolverà il suo dilemma?

M. Col solito compromesso: andremo sul lago di Garda.

G. Ma allora sai che pesci pigliare: pesci d'acqua dolce!

M. Tu, piuttosto, che programma hai?

G. Io? Niente di preciso. Andrò un po' in giro. Forse ritornerò a Ravenna, che non vedo da diversi anni.

L. Come, dottore? Ma ci va circa una volta al mese per affari!

G. Appunto, signorina. Ci *vado*, ma non la *vedo*. Ho sempre tanto da fare che non riesco mai a visitare i monumenti. E sa, i mosaici, bisogna guardarli bene, uno per uno!

Language Practice

1 Pattern sentences

La mensa è il posto dove mangiano gli impiegati della fabbrica.

La signorina Marzullo passerà tutto il pomeriggio in ufficio, per sbrigare la corrispondenza arretrata.

La signora Garbiati, moglie dell'ingegnere, vuole andare al mare; sua figlia in montagna.

Il dottor Giudice va a Ravenna circa una volta al mese per affari, e non per turismo.

2 La fabbrica produce motori elettrici? Sì, li produce.

Gli impiegati bevono il caffè?
La segretaria sbrigherà la corrispondenza?
La signorina Luisa scriverà le lettere?
La signorina Luisa visiterà i nonni?
Il dottor Giudice rivedrà i mosaici di Ravenna?

3 La signorina Luisa passerà un mese dai nonni.

Mio fratello ed io . . .
. . . sul lago di Garda.
. . . una quindicina di giorni . . .

4 Io conosco Ravenna, ma non ci ritorno da quando ero giovane.

. . . da qualche anno.
Il dottor Giudice . . .
. . . non ci passa una vacanza . . .
Mia moglie ed io . . .

Notes

The Future Tense

The future tense endings are added to the infinitive minus its final -*e*. Verbs with infinitives ending in -*are* change the *a* to *e*:

-ARE	parler-	ò
		ai
		à
-ERE	legger-	emo
		ete
-IRE	finir-	anno

parlare: parlerò, parlerai, parlerà etc.
leggere: leggerò, leggerai, leggerà etc.
finire: finirò, finirai, finirà etc.

CONTRACTED FUTURE

Some verbs, however, derive their future from a shortened or 'contracted' form of their infinitive. The most common are:

andare	andrò
avere	avrò
dovere	dovrò
potere	potrò
sapere	saprò
tenere	terrò
vedere	vedrò
venire	verrò
volere	vorrò

The future of *essere* is:

sarò
sarai
sarà
saremo
sarete
saranno

Unstressed Particles 1

Here is a first group of four object particles:

	Sing.		Plur.	
m.	*lo*	him	*li*	
		it		them
f.	*la*	her	*le*	

Bevi il latte?	Are you drinking your milk?
Sì, lo bevo	Yes, I'm drinking it
Chi sbriga la corrispondenza?	Who deals with the correspondence?
La sbriga la segretaria	The secretary deals with it
Dove sono i giornali?	Where are the newspapers?
Non li vedo	I can't see them
Le lettere sono pronte, dottore;	The letters are ready, Dr. Giudice;
le vuol firmare?	will you sign them?

The unstressed particles, which in English follow the verb, precede it in Italian, except when it is in the infinitive, imperative (cf. below) or gerund form:

Non la vedo	I don't see it/her

But:

Vogliono vedermi	They want to see me
Bisogna guardarli bene, uno per uno	One must look at them carefully, one by one

The same rules apply to *ci* (or *vi*) meaning 'there':

Ci vado una volta al mese	I go there once a month
Devo andarci	I must go there

Note that the infinitive drops its final -*e* before the particle which is joined to it to make a single word.

Forms of Command or Request

There are several ways of addressing a person in Italian, but only two are commonly used: the informal *tu*, which is used for someone with whom you would be on Christian name terms in English and always when addressing a child, and the formal *Lei* which is correct in all other cases. '*Dare del tu*' (to address someone informally) requires the use of the 2nd person singular of the verb (the pronoun *tu* itself is mostly omitted):

Che razza di consigli che dai alla mia segretaria!
What kind of advice are you giving to my secretary!

'*Dare del Lei*' (to address someone formally), on the other hand, requires the 3rd person singular of the verb, since *lei* is really a 3rd person singular pronoun:

Perchè non pensa alle prossime vacanze?
Why don't you think about the coming holidays?

In most cases the plural of both *tu* and *Lei* is *voi* (i.e. 2nd person plural form of the verb). (Cf., however, lesson 7 page 70).

Since there are two ways of saying 'you' in Italian, there are also two forms of command or request.

THE IMPERATIVE (Informal)

The imperative is identical with the present indicative, except for -*are* verbs, when the 2nd person singular ends in -*a*:

-ARE	(*tu*) *parli* you are speaking	*parla!* speak
	(*noi*) *parliamo* we are speaking	*parliamo!* let's speak
	(*voi*) *parlate* you are speaking	*parlate!* speak
-ERE	(*tu*) *leggi* you are reading	*leggi!* read
	(*noi*) *leggiamo* we are reading	*leggiamo!* let's read
	(*voi*) *leggete* you are reading	*leggete!* read
-IRE	(*tu*) *parti* you are leaving	*parti!* leave
	(*noi*) *partiamo* we are leaving	*partiamo!* let's leave
	(*voi*) *partite* you are leaving	*partite!* leave

Unstressed particles are joined to the end of the imperative to make a single word:

lo leggi you are reading it	*leggilo!* read it
lo leggiamo we are reading it	*leggiamolo!* let's read it
lo leggete you are reading it	*leggetelo!* read it

THE FORM OF POLITE REQUEST (Formal)

This form, used for people one would address as *Lei*, is borrowed from the present tense of the subjunctive (see table):

Signorina . . . immagini di non essere in ufficio, cominci a fantasticare
Pretend you're not in the office, start day dreaming

PRESENT SUBJUNCTIVE OF VERBS ENDING IN -*are*, -*ere*, -*ire*

-ARE: pensare	-ERE: mettere	-IRE: partire
pens- i	mett- a	part -a
pens- i	mett- a	part -a
pens- i	mett- a	part -a
pens- iamo	mett- iamo	part -iamo
pens- iate	mett- iate	part -iate
pens- ino	mett- ano	part -ano

Some verbs in -*ire*, like *finire*, have -*isc*- before the endings of the three persons of the singular and the 3rd person plural.

Unstressed particles are not joined to the subjunctive, but always precede it:

lo legga!   read it

Che and *chi*

It is important to avoid confusion between these two words.

Che is a multi-purpose word, rather like 'that' in English. (C.f. also page 94)

It means 'what' in exclamations:

Che tempo magnifico!
What wonderful weather!

It can refer to both people and things:

Beata Lei che non ha problemi!
Lucky you who have no problems!
Il film che ho visto ieri era molto bello
The film that I saw yesterday was very good

It may also be used to join two clauses:

Ho tanto da fare che non riesco mai a visitare i monumenti
I have so much to do that I never manage to see the monuments

Chi is used in questions, and can only refer to people:

Chi sbrigherà tutta la corrispondenza?
Who will get through all the correspondence?

Chi can also mean 'whoever' or 'he who' as in the proverb:

Chi ha la casa di vetro non tiri sassi al vicino
People who live in glass houses shouldn't throw stones

Remember that it is important in Italian always to pronounce the final vowel clearly. This may help to avoid confusion between *che* and *chi*.

Uses of *da*

The most usual meaning of *da* is 'from':

| *Riceverò un libro da mio zio* | I shall receive a book from my uncle |
| *Compro il formaggio da Canova* | I buy cheese from Canova |

Da also means 'at or to the shop or house' of a named person:

Compro il formaggio da Canova	I buy cheese at Canova's
Passo le vacanze dai nonni	I spend my holidays at my grandparents'
Vado dal farmacista	I am going to the chemist's

Remember to use *in* and not *da* with the name of the place itself:

in farmacia   at the chemist's shop

Da means 'since' or 'for' in sentences indicating the passing of time:

Non vedo i nonni da qualche anno, dal 1965
I haven't seen my grandparents for some years, since 1965
Vivo in Inghilterra da sei anni
I have been living in England for six years

Notice that in Italian the present tense is used (*vedo, vivo*) because the situation, although beginning in the past, is still continuing in the present.

Do not confuse *da* with *dà* ('he/she gives', from the verb *dare*).

Possessives 1

The possessives are:

	my mine	your yours	his her(s)	our(s)	your(s)	their(s)
S. m.	mio	tuo	suo	nostro	vostro	
f.	mia	tua	sua	nostra	vostra	
Pl. m.	miei	tuoi	suoi	nostri	vostri	loro
f.	mie	tue	sue	nostre	vostre	(invariable)

They agree with the thing possessed and not with its owner. For the reason why *tua moglie* and *tuo figlio* are not preceded by the definite article cf. lesson 4 page 42, where possessives are treated in greater detail. Very often the possessives are omitted in Italian where they would be used in English:

Andrò per un mesetto in Puglia, dai nonni
I'll go for a month to Puglia to stay with my grandparents

Nouns in -*nza*

Many Italian nouns ending in -*nza* are similar to English words ending in -nce or -ncy:

la corrispondenza arretrata	the backlog of correspondence
amano l'indipendenza	they love independence

Here are a few more examples:

l'ambulanza militare	the military ambulance
che strana coincidenza!	what a strange coincidence!
una grande distanza	a great distance
alta frequenza	high frequency
uno stato di emergenza	a state of emergency
mostrare indifferenza	to show indifference
provare l'innocenza di qualcuno	to prove somebody's innocence
presenza di spirito	presence of mind
l'arte e la scienza	art and science
c'è troppa violenza nella nostra società	there is too much violence in our society

All Italian words ending in -*nza* are feminine and indicate an abstract idea or notion.

Text Notes

mensa – canteen of a factory, refectory or army mess

elettrodomestici – electric household appliances
This includes such things as *lavatrici* – washing machines, and *frigoriferi* – refrigerators.

le due del pomeriggio – 2 p.m.
The article is feminine plural because *ore* is understood.

comincia a far caldo
Remember the idiomatic use of the verb *fare* when talking about the weather: *fa bel tempo* – the weather is fine, *fa caldo* – it's hot, *fa freddo* – it's cold etc. The final -*e* of the infinitive ending is often dropped (cf. *dovremo star chiusi*).

ecco fatto! – there you are! (lit. here, it's done)
This is an expression indicating that something has been done quickly and promptly.

andiamo . . . via! – come, come!

che razza di consigli! – what sort of advice!

castelli in aria – castles in Spain (lit. in the air)

non stia in pensiero – don't worry

niente
It can be used in two ways: (1) as an equivalent of the English 'no': *niente fantasie* – no flights of fancy, *niente birra* – no beer, *niente famiglia tra i piedi* – no family in the way; and in this case no verb is required; (2) as an equivalent of 'nothing'. When followed by an adjective it always takes *di*: *niente di preciso* – nothing definite, *niente di strano* – nothing strange, *niente di buono* – nothing good.

bell'e fatto – all ready, ready made

un mesetto
The ending -*etto* added to expressions of time means 'about': *un mesetto* – about a month, *un annetto* – about a year, *un'oretta* – about an hour.

è da qualche anno che non ci vado = non ci vado da qualche anno – I haven't been there for a few years
Qualche meaning 'some', 'a few' is invariable and is always followed by a singular noun.

beata Lei! – lucky you!

in montagna – to the mountains
In other contexts this could mean 'in the mountains'. The use of prepositions in Italian such as *in*, *da*, *a* etc., may not necessarily be the same as that of their English equivalents.

non so che pesci pigliare – I don't know what to do (lit. I don't know what fish to catch)

per conto suo – on his own (account)

chissà = chi sa – who knows
When two words are put together the initial consonant of the second word is often doubled (cf. *piuttosto* – rather, from *più + tosto*).

dilemma, programma
Remember that these two nouns, and several others ending in *-ma* (e.g. *tema* – theme, essay, *problema* – problem, *sistema* – system, *telegramma* – telegram etc.) are masculine and form their plural in *-i*.

acqua dolce – freshwater
Its opposite is *acqua salsa* or *acqua di mare* – sea-water.

come, dottore? what do you mean, Dr. Giudice?
Italians use academic and technical titles much more than the English. All university graduates are called *dottore*, and graduates in any branch of engineering are called *ingegnere*. When addressing the person directly, the title is not followed by the surname of the person, and this also applies to *signore, signorina* and *signora*:
Andiamo, signorina! Via . . . – Come, come Miss Marzullo!
When these titles are followed by a surname, i.e. when talking about a person, the final *-e* of the title is dropped:
Il dottor Giudice va a Ravenna – Dr. Giudice is going to Ravenna

una volta al mese – once a month

uno per uno (also *ad uno ad uno*) – one by one

Programmi per le vacanze *Summary*

Nella mensa della Ditta Felice Cossogno & Figli, tre persone parlano delle prossime vacanze.

I piani della signorina Luisa Marzullo, segretaria dell'ufficio commerciale, sono bell'e fatti. Passerà un mesetto in Puglia, dai nonni. È da qualche anno che non ci va, e loro vogliono assolutamente vederla quest'estate.

Il dottor Giudice, vice-direttore dell'ufficio commerciale, ritornerà a Ravenna in vacanza. Vuole visitare i monumenti, specialmente i mosaici.

L'ingegner Garbiati, direttore tecnico, non sa che pesci pigliare. Sua figlia vuole andare al mare, sua moglie in montagna. E così l'ingegnere risolverà il problema con un compromesso: tutti andranno a passare le vacanze sul lago di Garda.

Sirmione, castello e porto

The lake of Garda is the largest of the Italian lakes and covers an area of about three hundred and seventy square kilometres. Its shape is rather like an elongated triangle, very narrow at one end, gradually widening towards the other. On the northern side of the lake rise mountains and hills covered in olive trees. On the southern side the countryside is more gentle. The wide southern part is split into two bays, Desenzano and Peschiera, by the narrow peninsula of Sirmione. The peninsula is two and a half miles long and in places no more than a hundred and thirty yards wide. Houses are scattered along the shore and are surrounded by olive trees. Sirmione has a very fine castle, the Scaliger Castle, which was built in 1250, and there are Roman remains said to be the villa of Catullus. At Salò the Riviera of Garda begins, stretching for ten miles as far as Gargnano. Gardone Riviera is the principal resort on the Riviera. Today one of its chief attractions is the Vittoriale degli Italiani, the residence of Gabriele D'Annunzio, where relics and mementoes of the poet are preserved. D'Annunzio donated the property to the Italian people in 1930.

Limone is a typical fishing village built at the foot of high steep walls of rock and surrounded by olive groves and citrus gardens arranged in terraces on the hill-slopes.

Malcesine stands on a small cape at the foot of Monte Baldo, just below the steep rocky height topped by Scaliger Castle with its great tower thirty-three metres high.

Garda has a very mild climate, and the vegetation, Mediterranean in type, is unusual for its position. Olives, oranges, lemons, oleanders and palm trees thrive here. The water of the lake is of a very deep blue and one of the many stories told is of a sunken city to be seen below.

The Scaliger family, who built the castles on the lake of Garda, were once the rulers of Verona, which can be easily reached from the lake. The Amphitheatre, called the Arena, has been very well preserved, and in summer open-air per-formances of operas are given there. Once every year there is a performance of a Shakespeare play, the first night traditionally by candlelight. In Verona Romeo and Juliet exist as historical characters. They lived in the early years of the 14th century, and there is a tomb which is claimed to be that of Juliet. Italians, when referring to the story, always put Juliet first and say: *Giulietta e Romeo*.

The Piazza delle Erbe is oblong in shape, a reflection of the forum of Roman Verona. At one end of the square is a column upon which stands the Lion of St. Mark, a reminder that Verona was governed for many years from Venice after the Scaliger family died out in the 15th century.

Una gita in barca

È una bella giornata di sole, ma non fa troppo caldo. Sono circa le undici di mattina. L'ingegner Garbiati, sua moglie e la loro figlia Carla, stanno percorrendo in automobile un tratto della strada che da Riva del Garda scende verso Gargnano. Questa strada è stretta e tortuosa e costeggia il lago. Adesso si avvicinano al paesino di Limone. L'ingegnere è al volante. Carla è seduta al suo fianco. La signora Pina è semisdraiata sul sedile posteriore.

CARLA Meno male che non fa troppo caldo. A Milano in questi ultimi giorni non se ne poteva proprio più. Qui invece si sta bene.

PINA Io non sto affatto bene, con questa strada tutta curve. Mario, che ne dici di fermarti fra poco?

MARIO Tra pochi minuti saremo a Limone e potremo fermarci lì.

C. Guarda papà che stupendi terrazzi coperti di pini e di olivi.

M. Non sono pini, sono cedri del Libano. E gli alberi bassi sono limoni: perciò il paese si chiama così.

P. Per amor del cielo, Carla, non distrarre papà mentre sta guidando.

C. Non ti preoccupare, mamma: papà guida benissimo. E poi, siamo quasi arrivati . . .

              *   *   *

M. Che ne dite di una gita in barca? C'è lì un uomo che ne ha da noleggiare.

C. Com'è graziosa quella bianca e nera! La prendiamo?

P. Va bene, una gita in barca, ma chi rema?

M. Remo io. Oggi son pieno di energia. E poi una buona remata prima di mangiare mi farà da aperitivo.

C. Faremo a turno. Un po' tu, un po' io, un po' la mamma.

P. Oh, per me potete remare sempre voi! È un piacere che vi lascio volentieri . . .

              *   *   *

P. Guarda com'è pittoresco il castello di Malcesine.

C. Dov'è? Non lo vedo.

P. Non lo vedi? Proprio di fronte. Mario, tieni la barca diritta, altrimenti lo perdiamo di vista . . .

C. Ma no! Stai facendo andar la barca a zig-zag!

M. Oh bella! Criticare è facile per i fannulloni. Perchè non vieni a remare tu, invece di star lì a dormire?

C. Io non sto dormendo, sto guardando il panorama e sto prendendo il sole . . . Mamma, per piacere, mi passi la crema solare? . . .

M. Proprio nessuno vuol dare il cambio a un pover'uomo che rema già da mezz'ora?

P. Chi era pieno di energie mezz'ora fa, e voleva remare come aperitivo?

C. Su, adesso remo io, altrimenti papà avrà tanto appetito che divorerà tutto il cestino.

Language Practice

1 Pattern sentences

L'ingegner Garbiati, sua moglie Pina e la loro figlia Carla, vanno in automobile al paesino di Limone.

Mario, Pina e Carla Garbiati vanno a fare una gita sul lago di Garda, in una barca bianca e nera.

Carla sta prendendo il sole e non vuole dare il cambio a suo padre che rema da mezz'ora.

2 Carla prende il sole.   Carla sta prendendo il sole.

Noi studiamo l'italiano.
Io parlo italiano.
Che cosa fa Mario?
Mario rema.
Sua moglie e sua figlia dormono.

3 Sta qui, Carla.   Non stare qui, Carla.

Andiamo a Limone.
Carla, dormi.
Mario, prendi la barca bianca e nera.
Mario, prendila.
Mario, fermati.
Carla e Pina, remate.

Notes

Uses of *Stare*

The verb *stare* has the basic meaning of 'to stay', 'to be in a place':

Oggi devo stare a casa   Today I must stay at home

The past participle of *stare* is *stato*, which is also used as the past participle of *essere*:

Sono stato a Milano   I have been to Milan

For the past participle cf. lesson 3, page 34.

Stare may be followed by *a* and an infinitive, when it indicates that the action is being performed without breaks or changes of place:

Papà sta a remare da mezz'ora   Father has been sitting there, rowing,
                                    for half an hour

State a sentire   Listen!
Che cosa stiamo a fare qui?   What are we staying here for?
Stiamo a vedere che cosa succede We're waiting to see what happens

In conjunction with a verbal form called 'gerund' (see below), *stare* takes on an 'auxiliary' function (i.e. in which it is used only to form tenses of other verbs and loses its own basic meaning).

The gerund is invariable and is formed by replacing the infinitive endings as follows:

-ARE verbs take -*ando*	remare	rem*ando*
-ERE } verbs take -*endo*	prendere	prend*endo*
-IRE }	dormire	dorm*endo*

Bere, *dire* and *fare* are contracted infinitives and form their gerunds from the fuller infinitive which has otherwise disappeared from the language.

Infinitive	Obsolete Infinitive	Gerund
bere	bevere	bevendo
dire	dicere	dicendo
fare	facere	facendo

When it combines with *stare* the Italian gerund corresponds to the English present participle in -ing:

Non distrarre papà mentre sta guidando
Don't distract your father while he's driving
Io non sto dormendo, sto guardando il panorama
I am not sleeping, I am looking at the view

The present tense of *stare* and the gerund stresses the fact that the action is continuing at the very moment of speaking. It should, however, be noted that the two English sentences might also be translated into Italian with the simple present:

Non distrarre papà mentre guida
Io non dormo, guardo il panorama

Unstressed Particles 2

REFLEXIVE CONSTRUCTION

With many English verbs it is not always necessary for the object to be expressed. Instead of 'He washes himself' for example, we can simply say 'He washes'. In Italian, however, the object (in this case 'himself') must be expressed by one of a further group of unstressed particles:

	Sing.	Plur.
1	mi	ci
2	ti	vi
3	si	si

Mario si lava	Mario washes (himself)
Mi diverto	I am enjoying myself
Potremo fermarci lì	We'll be able to stop there

Like the other particles we saw in lesson 1, page 14, they always precede the verb unless it is in the imperative, infinitive or gerund form.
When these particles are the only object of a verb, as in the above examples, they are known as 'reflexives'.

In some cases, however, verbs may take two objects, one of which is an unstressed particle:

Mi passi la crema solare?

It then becomes important to distinguish between the indirect object (expressed in this case by the particle) and the direct object of the verb:

Will you pass *me* (ind. obj.) *the sun lotion* (dir. obj.)

Here *mi* is not the reflexive 'myself' but the indirect object 'to me'.

Mi, ti, ci, vi are used both as direct and indirect objects, and as reflexives.

THE PARTICLE *ne*

This particle follows the same position rules as all the others. It means approximately: 'of' or 'about what has just been mentioned', or 'from the place just mentioned'.

Ne parleremo domani
We'll talk about it tomorrow
Sei stato dal farmacista? Ne ritorno ora
Have you been to the chemist's? I'm just coming back from there

Often *ne* refers to something which is just about to be mentioned, and requires no translation in English:

Che ne dite di una gita in barca?   What would you say to a boat trip?

When other particles ending in *-i* are followed by *ne*, they change their ending to *-e*:

Te ne parlerò domani   I'll talk to you about it tomorrow
Non se ne poteva proprio più   One could not stand it any longer

IMPERSONAL *si*

Si, as well as being the reflexive particle translating 'himself, herself, itself, themselves', is also used in a special construction where the subject of the verb is not a specified person.

Qui si parla inglese   English is spoken here

There is no precise equivalent to this construction in English, and it is usually translated either by the passive (as above) or by 'one' or 'people' as subject:

Qui si sta davvero bene   One is quite comfortable here
                                      (or This is fine!)

Negative Forms of Command and Request

The negative of the imperative in the singular (*tu* form) is *non* followed by the infinitive:

Parla!   Speak
Non parlare!   Do not speak

In the plural, it is *non* followed by the appropriate form:

Non andiamo via   Let's not go away
Non disturbate   Don't disturb

Normally the unstressed particles come after the imperative (cf. lesson 1 page 15), but in the negative imperative they can either come before it or be joined to the end:

Non ti preoccupare
or
Non preoccuparti } Don't worry

Non lo guardate
or
Non guardatelo } Don't look at him/it

The negative of the form of polite request is simply formed by putting *non* before the form of polite request:

Non si preoccupi

Prima

'Before' followed by a verb (as in 'before going' etc.) is in Italian *prima di* followed by the infinitive (*prima di andare*):

Una buona remata prima di mangiare mi farà da aperitivo
A good row before eating will give me an appetite
(lit. will act as an apéritif)

More uses of *da*

Da followed by an infinitive or by a noun without the article, indicates the use or purpose of the thing mentioned:

acqua da bere	drinking water
barche da noleggiare	boats for hire
un cestino da viaggio	a packed lunch
	(lit. a (food) basket for travel)
una macchina da cucire	a sewing machine

Personal Pronouns 1

	Sing.	Plur.
1	io	noi
2	tu	voi
3 m.	(egli) lui	(essi) loro
f.	(ella) lei	(esse)

(The pronouns between brackets in the table above are seldom used in the spoken language)

Personal subject pronouns are not normally necessary in Italian, since the verb endings always show quite clearly who the subject is. They must, however, be used when special clarity, emphasis or contrast are needed:

Io non sto affatto bene	*I* am not feeling at all well
Chi rema? Remo io	Who's going to row? *I* am
Perchè non vieni a remare tu,	Why don't *you* row,
invece di dormire?	instead of sleeping?
Io non sto dormendo	*I* am not sleeping

In English this emphasis is rendered by voice stress. Note that subject pronouns often come after the verb.

Text Notes

semisdraiata – reclining (lit. half lying down)

Semi-, in combination with adjectives or nouns, has the same meaning as in English: *semicerchio* – semicircle, *semifinale* – semifinal, *semitono* – semitone etc.

meno male che . . . – thank goodness . . .

io non sto affatto bene – I don't feel at all well (*non* . . . *affatto* – not at all)

fra poco . . . *tra pochi minuti* – in a short while, in a few minutes' time

Either *tra* or *fra* may be used, depending on which sounds better in the sentence: *tra* (or *fra*) *pochi minuti* – in a few minutes, but *fra tre ore* – in three hours' time, Note that in the first sentence *poco* is an adverb and therefore appears in its invariable form; in the second it is an adjective and agrees with *minuti*.

bianca e nera – black and white

Note that the order in which these adjectives appear together is always the reverse of the English one.

remo io . . . *una buona remata*

There are many nouns ending in *-ata* (fem. sing.) connected with verbs or other nouns. Here are a few examples with their meanings:

Those derived from verbs in *-are*: they imply that the action expressed by the verb is being done at some length:

una chiacchierata	a chat
una camminata	a walk, a hike
una passeggiata	a stroll, a walk
una mangiata	a square meal
una sgridata	a reprimand

Those derived from other nouns:
(a) a blow or a hit by means of . . .

una coltellata	a stab
una martellata	a hammer blow
una pedata	a kick

(b) a . . . -ful

una boccata	a mouthful
una cucchiaiata	a spoonful
una bracciata	an armful

(c) behaving like a . . .

una bambinata	a childish action
una stupidata	foolish behaviour
una birichinata	a prank

faremo a turno – we'll take it in turns

un po'

The apostrophe indicates that it is a shortened form of *un poco* – a little.

per me – as far as I'm concerned

altrimenti lo perdiamo di vista – otherwise we'll lose sight of it

oh bella!

Italian idiom expressing impatience and irritation, as in this case ('I like that!'), or astonishment ('well I never, fancy that!').

fannullone – idler, lazibones (from *fare* – to do and *nulla* – nothing)

dare il cambio a qualcuno – to relieve someone

un pover'uomo

This is not the same as *un uomo povero*: the former means 'a poor wretch', the latter 'a man without money' (cf. lesson 7, page 70).

Una gita in barca *Summary*

La famiglia Garbiati percorre in automobile la strada stretta e tortuosa che costeggia il lago di Garda, tra Riva e Gargnano.

Intorno ci sono stupendi terrazzi, coperti di limoni e cedri del Libano.

I Garbiati si fermano a Limone. Il tempo è bello e l'ingegnere noleggia una bella barca bianca e nera per fare una gita sul lago. Pensa che una buona remata prima di pranzo gli farà da aperitivo.

Sua moglie e sua figlia preferiscono prendere il sole e guardare il panorama. Ma dopo mezz'ora l'ingegnere comincia ad essere stanco, e Carla decide di dare il cambio a suo padre: altrimenti egli avrà tanto appetito che divorerà tutto il cestino!

3 Ravenna

Before Venice was heard of, Ravenna existed as a lagoon city, a city of marshland whose streets were canals and whose people travelled by boat or barge. Gradually the tide ebbed away, leaving Ravenna an inland town, although a canal five miles long still connects it to the sea. Once one of the most important cities in Italy, its prosperity began when it became the capital of the Western Roman Empire, the imperial court transferring from Milan in 403. Later in the same century the king of the Goths, Theodoric, made it the principal city in his Italian kingdom and then, in 539, it fell into the hands of the Byzantines. All this happened in the space of a century and a half, but this was sufficient to ensure Ravenna a lasting place in the history of world art. Nowhere else in Europe can one find such important relics of the 5th and 6th centuries, the earliest period of Christian art.

Many buildings were erected during this period and many were decorated with mosaics: the tomb of Galla Placidia for instance, who was a Roman empress, is completely covered, floor, walls and ceiling, with decorations dating from the year 446. The church of San Vitale was begun in the reign of Theodoric but consecrated in 547 when Ravenna was under the rule of the Byzantines. Octagonal in shape, it has mosaics as old as the church itself. Those showing the Byzantine Emperor Justinian and the Empress Theodora and her court are the most famous.

About three miles from Ravenna is the church of Sant'Apollinare in Classe, the last relic of the thriving naval port which Augustus established. Beyond the church is the pinewood – *la pineta*, which Dante loved and which he called: *la divina foresta spessa e viva*. Dante sought refuge in Ravenna when he was exiled from Florence and spent the last few years of his life there. When he died, the people of Ravenna had a great deal of trouble keeping his remains in their city, since the Florentines were now repentant and dearly wished to have them. In 1519 envoys from Florence arrived with a papal injunction demanding that the people of Ravenna should surrender the great poet's remains. This they were not disposed to do and so they hid them in a safe place, but so well did they hide them that later when they came to look for them, even they could not find them. They were only discovered quite by chance some three hundred and fifty years later, and Ravenna has carefully and jealously guarded this envied treasure ever since.

Like Dante, Byron too loved the pinewood of Ravenna, often riding there in the evenings. Now the wood is much less dense than it was in Dante's, or even in Byron's, time. It is here that the white sands of the important fishing port of Ravenna Marina begin. It is famous for its *brodetto alla ravennate*, *brodetto* being the name given to fish soup along the coast of the Adriatic. The fish used are squid (*seppie, calamaretti* or *calamaroni*), eel, red mullet, sole and *cannocchie* – a flat-tailed Adriatic fish. The soup and the fish are served at the same time, but in separate dishes.

Il vecchio cameriere

Il palazzo comunale di Ravenna, in Piazza del Popolo, è del Quattrocento. Come molti edifici del genere nell'Italia del nord, ha un bel portico dove la gente può ripararsi dalla pioggia, o, come oggi, dal sole.

Sotto quel portico ci sono i tavolini di un caffè. Il dottor Giudice è seduto ad uno di quei tavolini, e sfoglia un giornale. Ai piedi ha una borsa rettangolare di cuoio giallo. Un cameriere si avvicina dopo qualche minuto.

CAMERIERE Il signore desidera?

GIOVANNI GIUDICE Un buon caffè, e un bicchiere d'acqua minerale. Bella fredda, eh?

C. Subito, signore.

G. Lei è nuovo qui?

C. Sì, signore. Sono venuto a Ravenna un mese e mezzo fa.

G. Allora Lei non è di Ravenna?

C. No. Prima abitavo a Napoli.

G. La signora Franchi c'è questa mattina?

C. La proprietaria? Se non c'è ancora, arriverà a momenti . . . Anzi, sta arrivando proprio ora.

G. Paola!

PAOLA FRANCHI Caro Giovanni! Quando sei arrivato? Ancora affari?

G. No. Sono arrivato ieri sera, questa volta da turista. E come vedi, son già qui a prendere il caffè. . . . C'è un nuovo cameriere: cosa è successo al buon Sartori?

F. Povero Sartori, ha resistito a lungo, ma in questi ultimi tempi non riusciva più a muoversi, con quell'artrite che ha.

G. Cosa fa ora? È a riposo?

F. No. Sai quel piccolo bar che ho aperto in via Fanti? L'ho mandato lì come gestore. Così è contento lui, perchè lavora seduto alla cassa; e sono contenta io perchè Sartori è una persona di fiducia.

G. Bene. Siccome devo andare a San Vitale, passerò di lì a salutarlo. Tanto è a due passi.

F. Cosa vai a fare a San Vitale?

G. Mia sorella mi ha scritto che stanno restaurando l'interno. Desideravo da tempo fotografare i mosaici; così ho scritto alla Sovrintendenza ai Monumenti chiedendo il permesso di approfittare delle impalcature.

F. E dove hai l'occorrente?

G. Tutto qui, in questa borsa: macchina fotografica, obbiettivi intercambiabili, treppiedi, lampo elettronico . . .

F. Sei bene attrezzato. Fotografi a colori?

G. A colori, naturalmente.

C. Permette, signore, ecco il suo caffè.

G. Grazie. Tenga pure il resto.

C. Grazie, signore.

G. Il cameriere è cambiato, ma il caffè sarà sempre uguale, spero?

F. Sempre quello di una volta. L'unica differenza è che ora è più caldo.

G. Perchè più caldo? Hai cambiato anche la macchina?

F. Ma no. Sartori ci metteva un'eternità dal banco al tavolino. Hai visto questo cameriere? Ci ha messo un decimo del tempo.

Ravenna, Basilica di San Vitale, interno

Language Practice

1 Pattern sentence

Sotto il portico del palazzo comunale di Ravenna in Piazza del Popolo, ci sono i tavolini di un caffè.

2 Io ho 3 fratelli. Lui quanti ne ha?   Ne ha 2.

Io ho 34 anni. Lui quanti ne ha?
Lui vuol comprare 12 libri. Tu quanti ne vuoi comprare?
Mio zio ha 56 anni. Il tuo quanti ne ha?
Io voglio mandare 10 cartoline. Voi quante ne volete mandare?
Mio nonno ha 88 anni. Il tuo quanti ne ha?
Noi passeremo 20 giorni al mare. Voi quanti ne passerete?

3 Ho già bevuto un caffè.   Questo è il secondo.

Hai già fatto 7 fotografie.
Abbiamo già visto 6 chiese.
Giovanni ha già fumato 5 sigarette.
Avete già visitato 3 musei.
Avete già fatto 2 lezioni.

4 Il dottor Giudice beveva un caffè   Anche ieri ha bevuto un caffè. *eh*
   ogni giorno.

Il dottor Giudice andava ogni giorno al bar.
Ogni giorno parlava con la proprietaria.
La signora Franchi arrivava alle 11 ogni giorno.
Il cameriere veniva ogni giorno a Ravenna per lavorare.
Ogni giorno ci metteva due ore.

5 Ho visto un bell'albergo.   Ho visto dei begli alberghi.

Ho mangiato un buon gelato.   *dei buoni gelati?*
Hai fotografato quel vecchio monumento?
Avete visto quello studente inglese?
Ho fatto una bella fotografia di San Vitale.
Stanno restaurando quell'edificio.

Notes

Counting: **Numbers** CARDINALS **and Numeral Adjectives** ORDINALS

CARDINALS

The numbers from 1 to 19:

uno, due, tre, quattro, cinque, sei, sette, otto, nove, dieci, undici, dodici, tredici, quattordici, quindici, sedici, diciassette, diciotto, diciannove

The tens from 20 to 90:

venti, trenta, quaranta, cinquanta, sessanta, settanta, ottanta, novanta

One hundred:

cento (invariable)

one thousand:

mille, pl. *mila*

(two thousand: *duemila*)

Neither *cento* nor *mille* are preceded by the article.

In counting remember that:

'and' is never translated into Italian:

duecento sessantaquattro   two hundred and sixty-four

In Italian we cannot say twelve hundred, thirteen hundred, etc.
We must say: *mille duecento, mille trecento*, etc.

The tens drop their final vowel before *uno* and *otto*:

mille quattrocento ottantatrè   1483
mille novecento sessantotto   1968

ORDINALS

Here are the first ten:

primo, secondo, terzo, quarto, quinto, sesto, settimo, ottavo, nono, decimo

All the others are formed by replacing the last vowel of the corresponding cardinal by the ending *-esimo*, with the exception of numbers ending in *-trè* (*-treesimo*) and *-sei* (*-seiesimo*) e.g. *quarantatrè: quarantatreesimo*.

quindici   quindicesimo
ventotto   ventottesimo

The ordinals are adjectives and follow the rules of agreement for adjectives.
Instead of applying the normal rule from *undicesimo* onwards it is also possible to say:

decimo primo, decimo secondo etc.

This applies especially to series of popes and kings:

Papa Giovanni ventesimo terzo   Pope John XXIII
(although *Papa Giovanni ventitreesimo* is much more common)

Centuries

It is perfectly correct to call the 13th century *il tredicesimo secolo*, but it is much more usual to say: *il Duecento*. Since the 13th century begins in 1200 (*mille duecento*), *il Duecento* becomes the term used for this century. The 14th century is *il Trecento*, and so on until the present century, which is *il Novecento*.

Adjectives in -ale

Many Italian adjectives (and nouns too) ending in -ale are similar to English adjectives in -al. Here are a few examples:

il regno animale	the animal kingdom
il colorante artificiale	artificial colouring
la stazione centrale	the central railway station
il sistema decimale	the decimal system
una strada laterale	a lateral (side) street
il palazzo ducale, episcopale	the ducal, episcopal palace
il governo locale, federale, neutrale	the local, federal, neutral government
la regola grammaticale	the grammatical rule
l'acqua minerale	mineral water
il festival annuale, musicale	the annual, musical festival
il quadro originale	the original picture
un caldo tropicale	a tropical heat
riforma sociale	social reform

The analogies between Italian and English words should help you to recognize their meaning when you hear or see them: but beware of italianizing English words! It may not work at all.

Quello, bello and *buono*

Quello and *bello* change their endings according to the same rules as the definite article:

il portico	il bel portico	quel portico
i portici	i bei portici	quei portici
l'albero	quell'albero	quel bell'albero
gli alberi	quegli alberi	quei begli alberi

Buono changes its endings in the singular like the indefinite article:

un caffè	un buon caffè	che buon caffè
il buon Sartori	un buono studente	una buona idea

In the plural *buono* behaves like other adjectives in -o.

The Past Participle

The past participle is formed as follows:

-ARE verbs replace their infinitive ending by -*ato*:

parlare	parlato
andare	andato

-IRE verbs replace their infinitive ending by -*ito*:

finire	finito
dormire	dormito

-ERE verbs need some caution, and we advise you to learn their past participle as each verb occurs. You will find these past participles either in the notes or in the vocabulary at the end of the book.

The past participle has the same forms as an adjective in -o.

Essere and *avere* as Auxiliary Verbs

Essere and *avere* are used in conjunction with the past participle to form certain tenses of verbs.

All verbs used reflexively and most verbs which cannot have an object have *essere* as their auxiliary. All other verbs have *avere*.

The Perfect and the Imperfect

THE PERFECT

This is formed with the present tense of the appropriate auxiliary verb and the past participle of the main verb.

If the auxiliary is *essere*, the past participle must agree with the subject of the sentence:

La Signora Franchi è venuta a trovarmi

Signora Franchi has come to see me.

Siamo arrivati ieri sera

We arrived last night

If the auxiliary is *avere* the past participle does not agree with the subject:

SIGNORA FRANCHI: *Ho aperto un piccolo bar in via Fanti*

I have opened a small café in via Fanti

Abbiamo visitato i mosaici di Ravenna

We have been to see the mosaics of Ravenna

THE IMPERFECT

This is formed by replacing the final *-re* of the infinitive ending by:

	-ARE	-ERE	-IRE	ESSERE	AVERE
-vo	desideravo	mettevo	riuscivo	ero	avevo
-vi	desideravi	mettevi	riuscivi	eri	avevi
-va	disiderava	metteva	riusciva	era	aveva
-vamo	desideravamo	mettevamo	riuscivamo	eravamo	avevamo
-vate	desideravate	mettevate	riuscivate	eravate	avevate
-vano*	desideravano	mettevano	riuscivano	erano	avevano

* In the 3rd person plural the stress moves from the last syllable but one to the last syllable but two, as in the present indicative.

USES OF THE IMPERFECT AND THE PERFECT

These are the two past tenses most used in spoken Italian and can best be understood by comparing and contrasting their use.

The perfect, like the English simple past, expresses something considered as finished or complete in itself at a definite point in time:

Sono venuto a Ravenna un mese fa	I came to Ravenna a month ago
L'ho mandato lì come gestore	I have sent him there as manager
Quando sei arrivato?	When did you arrive?

The imperfect, on the other hand, is used to emphasize continuity or repetition and the idea of completion is not so important. In most cases it describes states or habitual actions. It translates the English 'used to do' or 'was doing', but like the perfect it may also translate the English simple past:

Quando ero studente, andavo a Ravenna ogni mese
When I was a student, I used to go to Ravenna every month
Prima abitavo a Napoli
I lived in Naples before that.

The perfect and the imperfect are often found in the same sentence if it is necessary to contrast two conceptions of time:

Mentre parlavo con Paola, è arrivato il cameriere
While I was talking to Paola, the waiter arrived
Desideravo da tempo (continuous action) *fotografare i mosaici così ho scritto* (completed action) *alla Sovrintendenza ai Monumenti . . .*

I was wanting to take pictures of the mosaics, so I wrote to the Ministry of Works . . .

Not all expressions of state or duration, however, necessarily require the imperfect; *a lungo* for example may be preceded by the perfect to stress completion and not duration:

Povero Sartori, ha resistito a lungo, ma in questi ultimi tempi, con quella artrite che ha, non riusciva più a muoversi
Poor Sartori, he carried on for a long time (and he has now stopped), recently he was hardly able to move for that arthritis of his

Another use of *da*

Da is also used to introduce a word expressing the state or condition someone is in at a given time:

da turista	as a tourist
da studente	as a student (when I, you, he etc. was a student)
Si è comportato da disonesto	He behaved dishonestly

Idiomatic use of the Future

The future is sometimes used to convey an idea of uncertainty or possibility:

Il caffè sarà sempre uguale, spero
The coffee is just as it used to be, I hope
Non farà più il cameriere, ma dovrà pur muoversi
He may not be a waiter any longer, but he still has to move around
Quanti anni avrà?
How old would he be?

Text Notes

la gente – people

Gente, in spite of its seeming plurality, is grammatically singular: *molta gente* – many people.

qualche minuto

The singular noun following *qualche* (cf. lesson 1, page 18) must refer to something that can be counted, not to a mass or group of things, when *un po'* (*poco*) *di* . . . must be used. Compare: *qualche persona* but *un po' di gente* – some people; *qualche zolletta di zucchero* – some lumps of sugar, but *un po' di zucchero* – some sugar.

il signore (or *la signora*) *desidera?* – (standard formula) – may I help you?

bella fredda – nice and cold

Coffee in Italy is often served with a glass of cold water.

di Ravenna – from Ravenna

Note that *di* is normally used in Italian to indicate the place of birth or origin, unless the idea of 'coming from' is specified, in which case *da* is used: *il dottor Giudice è di Ravenna, ma viene da Milano; il cameriere viene da Napoli.*

a momenti – in a few moments, any minute now

cosa è successo al buon Sartori? – what's happened to good old Sartori?

è a riposo? – has he retired?

persona di fiducia – trustworthy person

salutare

Salutare has the basic meaning of 'to greet' and may be translated in different ways in English: *passerò di lì a salutarlo* – I'll go and say hello to him, *mi saluti sua sorella* – give my regards to your sister, *sono andato a salutarlo alla stazione* – I went to the station to say hello/to see him off.

tanto è a due passi – it's only a short distance anyway

Sovrintendenza ai Monumenti

The nearest British equivalent is the Ministry of Public Building and Works.

l'occorrente – the necessary (equipment)

This includes *obbiettivi intercambiabili* – interchangeable lenses, *treppiedi* – tripod, *lampo* (or *lampeggiatore*) *elettronico* – electronic flash (which most Italians call *flash* anyway!)

bene attrezzato – well equipped

tenga pure il resto – keep the change

sempre quello di una volta – the same as it always was

ci metteva . . . ci ha messo

A common Italian idiom for 'to take' (time): *quanto ci hai messo?* – how long did it take you? *non metterci troppo* – don't take too long.

Il vecchio cameriere *Summary*

Il dottor Giudice è ritornato a Ravenna in vacanza. In una borsa di cuoio giallo ha portato tutto l'occorrente per fare fotografie a colori dei mosaici di San Vitale: è molto bene attrezzato.

Per prima cosa è andato a prendere il caffè in Piazza del Popolo da una vecchia amica, la signora Paola Franchi, proprietaria del bar sotto i portici.

Il cameriere che lo serviva sempre non c'è più. La signora Franchi allora dice che il vecchio Sartori non riusciva quasi più a camminare a causa della sua artrite: così l'ha mandato a gestire un piccolo bar che ha aperto in via Fanti.

Ma, se il cameriere è cambiato, il caffè è sempre buono come quello di una volta.

Gubbio, Festa dei Ceri

4 L'Umbria

Umbria lies in the centre of Italy and has no coastline. Its countryside is soft and hilly like that of Tuscany, and many of its towns are built on the summits or slopes of hills. The Romans established stations in Umbria and built their Via Flaminia through the centre of it. Many of the towns have important Roman remains but their aspect is essentially medieval. During the Middle Ages, towns like Spoleto, Assisi and Gubbio were independent city states, constantly having to defend themselves against neighbouring towns as well as foreign armies.

Gubbio was once one of the largest and strongest of the Umbrian cities. Narrow lanes wind upwards between the grey stone houses to the Palazzo dei Consoli, the seat of government in the Middle Ages. As one climbs the hill, noise and the 20th century are left behind, and one steps back into the Middle Ages. The Palazzo dei Consoli was built in the 14th century, and towers two hundred feet above the surrounding houses, a symbol of the great strength this medieval city once had.

Assisi too was an independent city state, but more important, it was the birthplace of St. Francis, the patron saint not only of Assisi but also of Italy. Assisi today lives in the shadow of its saint, called *il Poverello*. The town is built high on the slopes of Monte Subasio, with the Basilica of San Francesco on the left, the castle above, and down below in the plain the church of Santa Maria degli Angeli, the Mother Church of the Franciscans. It was here on this site that the earliest Franciscans lived, in huts around a little chapel called the *Portiuncula* – 'the little portion', and it was here that St. Francis died. St. Francis himself had entreated his followers to build 'little churches', but the Basilica di San Francesco, built in his honour and to house his remains, is far from small. It is, in fact, two churches, one built on top of the other. Both are rich in frescoes, but the most famous are those by Giotto and his school in the Upper Church, showing scenes from the life of the saint.

In modern times these hill towns of Umbria have declined in power, and few of them have overflowed their medieval walls. Spoleto too, had been prosperous, like Gubbio, and then came the decline: There was no scope for the development of modern industry and the town's only wealth, though an important one, lay in its history and in the buildings reflecting that history. Then in 1957 Gian Carlo Menotti chose it as the setting for a festival of the arts (the Festival of Two Worlds), in which he wanted to harmonize the past and the present.

Umbrian towns have a great number of local festivals, most of them dating back to the earliest times of settlement, and many of them religious in origin. One of the most interesting of the local festivals is held in Gubbio. It is in honour of the Patron Saint, Ubaldo and is called the Festa dei Ceri, although *ceri* – 'candles', are not used. The *ceri* are in fact great wooden structures, twenty feet high. There are three of them, each surmounted by the emblem of a saint, and carried by twelve members of the guild under the saint's protection: St. Anthony is carried by the farm workers, St. George by the merchants and St. Ubaldo by the masons.

The three groups of men, called *ceraioli*, all dressed in white trousers with shirts of either red, yellow or black, run up the steep slope of Monte Ingino carrying the *ceri* which they deposit in the church of St. Ubaldo; there they are left until the following May when the festa will be held again.

Una fanatica dell'arte moderna

Bruno Peruzzi, dopo aver terminato gli studi tecnici, è stato assunto dalla Cossogno come disegnatore. Alla fine di giugno ha preso due settimane di vacanze per andare da suo zio a Spoleto.

Questa antica città dell'Umbria è diventata dal 1957, con la fondazione del Festival dei Due Mondi, un centro di arte moderna di fama internazionale.

Lo zio di Bruno abita in una graziosa villetta alle pendici del Monteluco. Ora sta per presentare il nipote all'amico Carlo Moretti e a sua figlia Lucia, invitati con altre persone ad un piccolo ricevimento.

ZIO Carlo, Lucia, ecco il mio nipote milanese Bruno Peruzzi, che volevo presentarvi.

LUCIA MORETTI Piacere.

BRUNO PERUZZI Molto lieto.

CARLO MORETTI Ah, Lei è Bruno. Ho conosciuto suo padre nel '64: come sta?

B. Sempre attivo, come al solito.

C. Mi fa piacere. Lo saluti da parte mia quando torna. E Lei quanto si trattiene?

B. Due settimane.

L. È venuto per il Festival, immagino?

B. Sì; ne conoscevo già la fama, e così quest'anno ho voluto venire a giudicare di persona.

L. Quali sono i suoi interessi artistici?

B. Oh, niente di approfondito: sono un tecnico ignorante, sa, e devo ancora farmi una cultura!

C. In questo ci diamo la mano. Perciò le dò un consiglio in confidenza: si guardi da mia figlia!

B. E perchè?

C. Perchè è una fanatica dell'arte moderna. Cercherà immediatamente di educarla, di trascinarla a teatri, concerti, mostre, o che so io, come tenta di fare con me da anni . . .

L. Esagerato!

C. La pura verità! . . . Mi scusi, Bruno, suo zio mi chiama. Devo lasciarla con Lucia. Non si lasci accalappiare, eh?

L. Non gli dia retta. Papà si diverte a mettermi in imbarazzo.

B. Ma no! Se è così, Lei è proprio la persona che fa per me. Spero che mi permetterà di accompagnarla a qualcuna delle manifestazioni.

L. Con piacere. Ha visto il programma?

B. L'ho in camera, ma ci ho appena dato un'occhiata.

L. Vedrà, è davvero ricco. Opera, prosa, musica sinfonica, balletto e dramma sperimentale, musica da camera, e poi mostre d'arte un po' dappertutto. Ce n'è per tutti i gusti.

B. Ho visto che ci sono dei buoni complessi . . .

L. . . . e degli eccellenti solisti, anche i meno noti. E poi ne arriva sempre qualcuno famoso. Qualche anno fa c'è stato Richter: un recital fantastico!

B. Attenda un attimo: vado a prendere il programma, così potremo vederlo insieme.

Spoleto, Duomo

L. Prego, faccia pure.
(*In moving across the room Bruno comes across Carlo Moretti who is talking to his uncle.*)
C. Ah, ah, ritirata strategica Bruno? Lucia l'ha già messo in fuga?
B. Al contrario, signor Moretti. Come Lei direbbe, mi sono lasciato accalappiare . . .

Language Practice

1 Pattern sentences

Bruno Peruzzi ha preso due settimane di vacanza per andare da suo zio che abita a Spoleto.

Bruno e Lucia stanno parlando del Festival dei Due Mondi che ha un bel programma di arte e di musica.

2 Hai visto il programma?   Sì, l'ho visto.
  Devi lasciare gli invitati?   Sì, li devo lasciare/Sì, devo lasciarli

  Ascolterai il concerto?
  Puoi accompagnare Lucia?
  Visiterete le chiese domani?
  Signorina, conosce già questa città?

3 Mandi il libro o il disco a tuo padre? Gli mando il libro.

  Hai dato il programma o i biglietti a Lucia?
  Servirete vermouth o whisky agli invitati?
  Offrirai un tè o un caffè a Bruno?
  Hai dato vino rosso o vino bianco a mia sorella?

4 Carla ha visto le sue zie.   Carla ha visto sua zia.

  Bruno ha visto i suoi fratelli.
  Luigi ha visto i suoi figli.
  I Garbiati hanno visto i loro cugini.
  Lucia ha visto le nostre amiche.
  Luisa ha visto i suoi zii.
  Piero ha visto le sue sorelle.

Notes

Possessives 2

Possessive adjectives in Italian agree with the thing possessed and not with its owner. In English my wife's watch is her (f.) watch; in Italian it is:

  il suo orologio; *suo* (m.) because *orologio* is masculine.

Loro is invariable and must always be preceded by an article:

  la loro villetta
  la loro figlia

The other possessive adjectives are normally preceded by an article. The definite article is, however, omitted when the possessives are followed by singular nouns indicating family relationships not qualified by another adjective or clause:

Ho conosciuto suo padre nel '64	I met your father in 1964
Si guardi da mia figlia	Beware of my daughter

But:

il mio nipote milanese	my nephew from Milan
il mio nipote che abita a Milano	my nephew who lives in Milan
i miei due cugini	my two cousins

The possessive adjectives can be preceded by *questo*, *quello* or by a number:

un tuo libro	one of your books/a book of yours
quel mio amico	that friend of mine
questa mia figlia	this daughter of mine

Stare 2

Stare per followed by an infinitive means: 'to be about to . . .'

Sta per presentare suo nipote all'amico
He is about to introduce his nephew to his friend
Stavo proprio per uscire
I was just about to go out
Sta per piovere
It's just about to rain/It's just going to rain

Per

Per followed by an infinitive normally indicates aim or purpose (except in the construction: *stare per . . .*)

Ha preso due settimane di vacanza per andare da suo zio
He has taken two weeks' holiday to go to his uncle's

Per has a similar meaning in:

È venuto per il Festival?
Have you come for the Festival? (i.e. *in order to* attend it)

Some Verbs used both reflexively and non-reflexively

Quanto tempo ti trattieni?	How long are you staying?
Lo zio mi ha trattenuto a cena	My uncle kept me for supper
Si guardi da mia figlia	Beware of my daughter
Guardi mia figlia	Look at my daughter
Non si lasci accalappiare	Don't let yourself be trapped
Devo lasciarla con Lucia	I must leave you with Lucia
Papà si diverte a mettermi in imbarazzo	Father enjoys embarrassing me
Questa commedia mi diverte	This comedy amuses me

Unstressed Particles 3

We have already met the 1st and 2nd person unstressed particles (*mi, ti, ci, vi*) which can be reflexive, direct or indirect object particles. The indirect object particles for the 3rd person singular, however, are: *gli* (masculine) and *le* (feminine).

Remember that the feminine is also used for the polite form of 'you':

Le ho dato un consiglio	I have given her (or you) some advice
Le ho scritto	I have written to her (or to you)

Gli is also being increasingly used as the 3rd person plural indirect object particle for both genders, instead of *loro*:

Non gli dia retta	Don't listen to him (or to them)

Here is a general table of all the unstressed particles:

		Reflexive	Direct Object		Indirect Object	
S.	1		mi			
	2		ti			
	3	si	m.	lo	m.	gli
			f.	la	f.	le
Pl.	1		ci			
	2		vi			
	3	si	m.	li		
			f.	le	m. & f.	gli – loro

Also: *ne* with the general meaning of 'of it', 'from there' etc.

and : *ci* and *vi* with the meaning of 'there'.

Another use of *da*

After a verb used in the passive, *da* means 'by':

È stato assunto dalla Cossogno come disegnatore
He has been taken on by the firm of Cossogno as a draughtsman (names of firms are considered feminine in Italian).

Plural of Nouns and Adjectives in *-ico*

If the tonic accent falls on the last syllable but two, these nouns and adjectives form their masculine plural in *-ici*:

artistico	artistici
fanatico	fanatici
tecnico	tecnici

But *carico* (load or laden) is an exception, forming its plural in *-ichi*.

All other nouns and adjectives in *-ico* form their masculine plural in *-ichi*:

fico (fig or fig tree)　　　　　　　　　　fichi

with a few exceptions such as:

amico (*amici*) and *nemico* (*nemici*).

Feminine plurals always end in *-che*:

fanatiche, tecniche, amiche etc.

Personal Pronouns 2

Note that *io* and *tu* have separate object forms: *me* and *te*.

	Singular			Plural		
	1st	2nd	3rd	1st	2nd	3rd
Subject	io	tu	m. (egli), lui f. (ella), lei			m. (essi) loro f. (esse)
				noi	voi	
Object	me	te	m. lui f. lei			loro

The object form is always used after prepositions and for emphasis and clarity:

Lei è proprio la persona che fa per me　You're just the person I need

Ci sono andato con te, non ricordi?　I went there with you,
　　　　　　　　　　　　　　　　　　　don't you remember?

Ha invitato me, non te　He's invited me, not you

Nouns in *-ista*

These nouns have the same ending in the masculine and feminine singular:

il pianista and *la pianista*

but the masculine ones form their plural in *-i* and the feminine, in *-e*:

i pianisti and *le pianiste*

Many of them correspond to English nouns in *-ist*:

Solisti di strumenti musicali	Soloists of musical instruments
il/la pianista	pianist
organista	organist
violinista	violinist
clarinettista	clarinettist
flautista	flautist
il/la dentista	dentist
conformista	conformist
imperialista	imperialist
pessimista	pessimist
ottimista	optimist
realista	realist
socialista	socialist
specialista	specialist

Text Notes

un piccolo ricevimento – a party

The English word party, however, is often used in Italy.

piacere . . . molto lieto (-a)

These may be thought of as shortened forms of *ho molto piacere/sono molto lieto (-a) di fare la sua conoscenza* – 'I'm very glad to meet you', and are the usual introduction formulae. The verb *conoscere*, as well as 'to know', means 'to get to know', 'to meet for the first time' (cf. lesson 11, page 102).

come al solito – as usual

festival . . . recital

Pronounce these as if they were Italian words, with the accent on the first syllable

devo ancora farmi una cultura – I still have to educate myself

in questo ci diamo la mano – we feel alike, we have something in common (lit. in this we shake hands)

è una fanatica dell'arte moderna – she's crazy about modern art

. . . o che so io – and Heaven knows what else

esagerato! – oh! nonsense (shortened form of *come sei esagerato* lit. 'how excessive you are')

dare retta a qualcuno – to listen, to pay attention to someone

Note that *retta*, is only used in this idiom with the meaning of 'attention'.

la persona che fa per me – just the person for me

manifestazioni

In this context 'spectacle', in a sports context 'fixture'. *Una manifestazione politica* is 'a political demonstration'.

l'ho in camera – I have it in my room

Note that articles and possessives are normally omitted in Italian before nouns indicating rooms in the house, places of work and generally places where one goes frequently or regularly: *la mamma è in cucina* – Mother is in the kitchen, *i bambini sono a scuola* – the children are at school, *vado in ufficio alle otto* – I go to the office at 8 a.m., *andiamo in chiesa ogni domenica* – we go to church every Sunday.

ci ho appena dato un'occhiata – I just glanced through it

Note that *ci* (here/there) often replaces *gli* or *le* when speaking of things or objects. (cf. *le ho appena dato un'occhiata* – I hardly gave her a look).

ce n'è per tutti i gusti – there's something for every taste

complesso – ensemble (mostly musical)

faccia pure – please do!

Una fanatica dell'arte moderna *Summary*

Bruno Peruzzi è un disegnatore che si interessa all'arte e alla musica, e non solo alle materie tecniche. Perciò ha preso due settimane di vacanza per andare al Festival dei Due Mondi, a Spoleto.

Qui è ospite di suo zio, che ha dato un piccolo ricevimento per gli amici. Bruno è molto lieto di fare la conoscenza di Lucia Moretti, che è tra gli invitati insieme al padre. Il signor Moretti si diverte a mettere la figlia in imbarazzo, e consiglia a Bruno di guardarsi da lei, perchè è una fanatica dell'arte moderna, e cercherà di trascinarlo a teatri, concerti e mostre.

Ma Bruno spera, al contrario, che Lucia gli permetterà di accompagnarla a qualcuna delle manifestazioni del Festival. Una ragazza che ha degli interessi artistici approfonditi è proprio la persona che fa per lui.

Marostica, partita a scacchi

5 Padova

Padova, Prato della Valle

Padua is easily reached by road or rail from Venice but one of the most pleasant routes is by the *burchiello*, the white steamer which runs along the Brenta, passing many of the country villas built by Venetian aristocrats when Venice was a wealthy and powerful sea-republic.

Padua itself is very old. There was a Roman city before the present one and Livy, it is said, was born there. Well-known to Elizabethan England, it was chosen by Shakespeare as his setting for *The Taming of the Shrew* and Portia claimed to be a lawyer from Padua. Generations of medical students in Shakespeare's time came to study at the medical school which was then the most famous in Europe. The University, which is called Il Bò because it was built on the site of an old inn with the sign of an ox, is still an important one today.

The Scrovegni Chapel was built in 1303 and was decorated by Giotto, whose famous frescoes tell the story of the lives of Christ and the Virgin and cover the whole building. Giotto came of a peasant family from Tuscany and was a friend of Dante, who probably stayed with him in Padua and came to the chapel to watch him at work.

Padua is called the city of a saint without a name, because the patron saint of Padua, St. Anthony, is always referred to by the people as simply: Il Santo. St. Anthony was a gentle saint rather like St. Francis and has become the patron saint of travellers and lost property. The Basilica which houses his tomb dwarfs all other buildings in Padua with its six Byzantine domes.

A few miles to the south-west of Padua are the Euganean Hills, well-known to Shelley and Byron. The hills have winding lanes and cart tracks and the villages on the slopes among the vines seem to be living in a past age. In the small village of Arquà there is the house where Petrarch lived. Abano, at the foot of the hills, is a spa which was much used by the Romans.

Near to Padua is the fortified town of Marostica where two important festivals are held. In June the Cherry Festival takes place in honour of the harvest which usually produces some of the best cherries in Italy. The main square of Marostica is paved like a chessboard, and in mid-September a very special game of chess is played with men in costume taking the parts of the king, bishop, knights and so on.

Palladio and Scamozzi were the two famous architects of this part of the Veneto and Vicenza, to the west of Padua, is remembered and visited principally because of Andrea Palladio whose birthplace it was and who designed many of its famous buildings. Born in 1518, he began work as a stonemason, but was later to design many of the villas of the Venetian aristocrats, as well as churches and town houses in Venice. Palladio's architecture appealed greatly to the English travellers who saw it and a new word, Palladian, came into the English language. The Earl of Burlington was a particular enthusiast, basing his villa at Chiswick on Palladio's villa La Rotonda. The Olympic Theatre in Vicenza was begun in 1580 by Palladio and completed by Scamozzi. It was probably the first covered theatre in Europe and is still in constant use. The seating is arranged in the form of semi-circles of steps, and the perspective of the stage is such as to give the impression of having considerable depth.

Una cura dimagrante

Lisa Bortolin, dattilografa nel reparto contabilità, ha accettato l'ospitalità di una zia paterna, proprietaria di una tabaccheria nel centro di Padova. Padova è una città ricca di arte e di storia, ma Lisa è più attirata dai divertimenti del Lido di Venezia, a poco più d'un'ora di viaggio, dove sperava di recarsi ogni giorno. Per diverse ragioni, le sue intenzioni non si sono pienamente realizzate, come potremo capire se ascoltiamo Lisa e sua zia che parlano a cena.

LISA Che buona cenetta, zia! Se non sto attenta qui divento una botte.

ZIA Si vede che l'aria di mare ti fa venire appetito.

L. Macchè, è la tua buona cucina! Tu, come fai a rimanere così magra?

Z. È un segreto personale . . . Dimmi un po', domani torni al Lido?

L. Non so . . . in fondo andarci ogni giorno è un po' monotono. Comincia a stancarmi.

Z. Sai, qui intorno a Padova c'è un'infinità di posti belli e interessanti. Potresti visitare Vicenza, i colli Euganei . . . Ascolta: va nelle Dolomiti; ci sono degli autobus che ne fanno il giro in una giornata.

L. Mah . . . dopotutto potrei anche passare una giornata tranquilla qui a Padova con te. Magari aiutarti un po' in tabaccheria . . .

Z. Se ne hai voglia, allora, fammi proprio questo piacere. Gina, sai, la mia commessa, stava poco bene questa sera, e le ho detto di rimanere a casa domani.

*　　　*　　　*

CLIENTE I Signorina, volevo delle cartoline illustrate della Cappella degli Scrovegni, ma non le vedo. Ce n'ha?

L. Guardi, ce ne devono essere lì a destra, vicino alla porta, tra quelle a colori.

CI. Ah, eccole qui. Ne prendo quattro. Quanto costano?

L. Quattro, a cinquanta lire l'una, fanno duecento lire.

CI. Vorrei anche dei francobolli per l'Inghilterra.

L. Per le cartoline ci vogliono 55 lire, e 90 per le lettere.

CI. Allora me ne dia quattro da 90 e dieci da 55.

L. Bene, signora. Con le cartoline illustrate fanno 1110 lire in tutto . . . Molte grazie. E Lei, signore, desidera?

CLIENTE II Due pacchetti di Nazionali esportazione, per favore.

L. Col filtro, o senza?

CII. Col filtro; e anche una scatoletta di cerini.

L. Eccole.

CII. Grazie.

L. Grazie a Lei. Arrivederla.

CII. Arrivederla.

*　　　*　　　*

L. Zia, dammi ancora un po' di risotto, per piacere.

Z. Ma come? Non avevi paura di diventare una botte?

L. Ieri sera sì. Ma oggi devo aver perduto almeno un chilo con tutto il lavoro che c'era da fare. Ce n'è davvero tanto in una tabaccheria; non l'avrei mai creduto: adesso capisco come fai a restare così snella.

z. Ora che hai scoperto il mio segreto, la prossima volta che vuoi fare una cura dimagrante, ti cedo il mio negozio per una settimana.
l. E tu, che cosa farai?
z. Io? Mi prenderò una vacanza al Lido di Venezia.

Language Practice

1 Lisa, invece di andare al Lido, aiuta sua zia, perchè c'è molto da fare.

   . . . rimane a casa . . .
   . . . perchè sta poco bene.
   . . . invece di fare un giro sulle Dolomiti . . .

2 La commessa vende quattro cartoline illustrate a una signora inglese.

   Lisa e sua zia . . .
   . . . a un signore francese.
   . . . sei pacchetti di sigarette . . .

3 Dimmi un po'.   Mi dica un po'.

   Guardalo bene.
   Facci un piacere.
   Vacci domani.
   Dalle dei cerini.
   Dammi cinque cartoline.
   Aiutami per favore.
   Prendine due.
   Non prenderle tutte.
   Portala via.
   Non portarla via.
   Ascoltalo adesso.
   Vieni qui.

4 Vuoi partire?   Sì, vorrei partire.

   Devi telefonare?
   Potete andare?
   Possono aiutare?
   Volete uscire?
   Dobbiamo ascoltare?
   Giorgio vuole partire?
   Puoi mandarlo?
   Devo venire?

5 Dove sono le cartoline?   Eccole.

   Dov'è il francobollo?
   Dove siete?
   Dove sono i bambini?
   Dov'è Gina?
   Dove sono le lettere?
   Dove sei?

Notes

Imperatives of one syllable

Some verbs, like *fare* and *dire*, have imperatives of one syllable in the *tu* form (2nd person singular):

fare	fa'
dire	di'
stare	sta
dare	dà
andare	va

All unstressed particles joined to them double their initial consonant, except obviously for *gli*:

Dimmi un po'	Tell me
Facci un piacere	Do us a favour
Dalle ancora un po' di risotto	Give her a little more risotto
Vacci domani	Go there tomorrow
Dagli un bacio	Give him a kiss

The Conditional

The conditional endings are:

scriver – *ei*
scriver – *esti*
scriver – *ebbe*
scriver – *emmo*
scriver – *este*
scriver – *ebbero*

To form the conditional, these endings are added to the infinitive in the same way as the future endings are (cf. lesson 1, page 13). Verbs forming their future from a contracted infinitive, form their conditional similarly:

dovere	dovrò	dovrei

The conditional of *essere* is:

sar – *ei*
sar – *esti* etc.

and of *avere*:

avr – *ei*
avr – *esti* etc.

The Past Tense of the Conditional (English: I should have . . .)

This is formed by using the conditional of *avere* or *essere* (cf. lesson 3, page 35) and the past participle of the verb.

Non l'avrei mai creduto	I would never have believed it
Saresti andato?	Would you have gone?

Prepositions used in counting

da indicates the value or rating of an article:

due francobolli da 90	two 90 lire stamps
Mi dia un pacchetto di sigarette da 20	Will you give me a packet of 20 cigarettes
un motore da 1100 *c.c.*	an 1100 c.c. engine

per is used in multiplying:

50 *per* 4 *fa* 200	50 times 4 is 200

Ecco

Ecco is used to call attention to something which is appearing or being shown: 'Look'; 'here is . . .'
All unstressed particles can be joined to *ecco*:

eccomi	here I am
eccoti	here you are
eccolo	here it is, here he is
eccola	here it is, here she is
eccoci	here we are
eccone due	here are two of them
eccotene due	here are two of them for you

The Present Subjunctive of a few Irregular Verbs

Remember that the form of polite request is borrowed from the subjunctive. For the present subjunctive of regular verbs cf. lesson 1, page 16.

ESSERE	AVERE	ANDARE	FARE
sia	abbia	vada	faccia
sia	abbia	vada	faccia
sia	abbia	vada	faccia
siamo	abbiamo	andiamo	facciamo
siate	abbiate	andiate	facciate
siano	abbiano	vadano	facciano

DARE	DIRE	TENERE	VENIRE
dia	dica	tenga	venga
dia	dica	tenga	venga
dia	dica	tenga	venga
diamo	diciamo	teniamo	veniamo
diate	diciate	teniate	veniate
diano	dicano	tengano	vengano

DOVERE	VOLERE	POTERE
deva	voglia	possa
deva	voglia	possa
deva	voglia	possa
dobbiamo	vogliamo	possiamo
dobbiate	vogliate	possiate
devano	vogliano	possano

Nouns ending in -*zione*

They generally correspond to English nouns ending in -tion, and are all feminine. Here are a few examples:

azione	action	*opposizione*	opposition
associazione	association (society)	*operazione*	operation
		posizione	position
attenzione	attention	*preoccupazione*	preoccupation
collezione	collection	*prevenzione*	prevention
condizione	condition	*protezione*	protection
cooperazione	cooperation	*reazione*	reaction
emozione	emotion	*situazione*	situation
intenzione	intention	*soluzione*	solution
invenzione	invention	*stazione*	station
lozione	lotion	*tradizione*	tradition
nozione	notion	*vaccinazione*	vaccination

Of course this does not apply to all English words ending in -tion: 'the ignition key' for example is *la chiave di accensione*; *esportazione* is simply 'export'.

Text Notes

una zia paterna – an aunt on her father's side

una tabaccheria

Italian tobacconists are licensed by the state to sell all articles produced under state monopoly, and these include stamps (for postage and stamp duties), salt and quinine, as well as tobacco and cigarettes. Most tobacconists also sell postcards, a limited range of stationery, smokers' requisites and some confectionery (throat pastilles, chewing-gum, sweets etc.). Some (*Bar-Tabaccheria*) also sell espresso-coffee and spirits.

se non sto attenta qui divento una botte – if I'm not careful I shall become a tub here

Note that in Italian the present tense is often used to express future ideas.

ti fa venire appetito – makes you hungry (lit. makes appetite come to you)

For more examples of this construction with *fare* cf. lesson 6, page 61.

macchè (or *ma che*)

Expression of denial, usually followed by repetition of what is being denied: *dove l'hai comprato? macchè comprato, l'ho fatto io stesso* – where did you buy it? I didn't buy it, I made it myself.

come fai a rimanere così magra? – how do you manage to keep so slim?

è un po' monotono – it's a bit boring

giornata

Whereas *giorno* is the day considered as a date or a point in time, *giornata* is the day considered as a length of time, as a working day, or from the point of view of the weather: *che giorno è oggi?* – what day is it today? but *che giornata!* – what a day! A similar distinction exists between *mattina* and *sera* and *mattinata* and *serata*.

54

magari aiutarti un po' – perhaps even help you a little

In this context *magari* means both 'even' and 'perhaps' whereas often it means one or the other: *magari andrò a Venezia domani* – perhaps I'll go to Venice tomorrow, *magari potresti arrivare fino alla tabaccheria* – you might even go as far as the tobacconist's. In other contexts it can express wishful thinking: *andresti volentieri a Venezia? magari!* – would you like to go to Venice? I wish I could! (or you bet!)

stava poco bene – she wasn't feeling very well

volevo delle cartoline illustrate

The imperfect of verbs expressing intention implies that such an intention has not been, or may not be, realized (I was hoping to buy picture postcards *but* I can't find them). It is therefore frequently used to 'tone down' requests: *volevo chiederle un piacere* – I'd like to ask you a favour (but perhaps you may not wish to grant it).

ce n'ha? = *ne ha?* – have you got any (there)?

It is not always possible to translate *ci* into English.

francobolli (often shortened to *bolli*) – (postage) stamps

(cf. compound nouns lesson 7, page 68).

ci vogliono 55 lire – you need 55 lire

In this expression the verb is singular or plural, according to the grammatical number of 'what is wanted': *ci vuole del sale in questo risotto* – this risotto needs salt, *per le cartoline con non più di cinque parole di saluti ci vogliono solo 25 lire* – postcards with no more than five words of greeting need only a 25 lire stamp.

Nazionali

The most common brand of Italian cigarettes: it comes in two varieties, *semplici* and *esportazione*. Connoisseurs believe that *esportazione* are better.

cerino

Italian wax matches, from *cera* – wax.

risotto

Common name for a variety of rice-based recipes typical of northern Italian cookery.

Una cura dimagrante *Summary*

La zia di Lisa Bortolin fa della buona cucina, eppure rimane sempre magra. Lisa, che sta molto attenta ad essere snella ed elegante, si preoccupa perchè a casa della zia mangia troppo.

All'inizio della sua vacanza a Padova, Lisa andava ogni mattina al Lido di Venezia, ma poi ha cominciato a stancarsi. La zia le ha suggerito molti posti belli e interessanti nei dintorni, che potrebbe facilmente visitare; ma Lisa ha pensato che dopotutto potrebbe anche restare una giornata a Padova, ad aiutare la zia nella sua tabaccheria in centro.

Quanto lavoro c'è da fare in tabaccheria! La gente viene continuamente a comprare sigarette, cerini, cartoline illustrate, francobolli e tante altre cose. La sera, a cena, Lisa mangia il buon risotto cucinato dalla zia con molto appetito. Ora ha capito come fa la zia a rimanere snella: lavorare molto è una buona cura dimagrante.

6 Pavia

The landscape of southern Lombardy is flat and gives the impression of un-limited fertility, the result of years of hard work on irrigation, making use of the waters of the Po. Large fields are divided by poplars, as characteristic of Lombardy as the cypress is of Tuscany.

The word 'Certosa', with its equivalent 'Chartreuse' in French and 'Charter-house' in English indicates a Carthusian monastery. The Certosa di Pavia, situated about five miles from the town of Pavia, is the most famous of these monasteries after the Mother House, the Grande Chartreuse near Grenoble. It must be one of the most costly monasteries ever built, both the Visconti and the Sforza families, the successive rulers of Milan, having spent vast amounts of money on it.

It was founded in 1396 by Gian Galeazzo Visconti, who had also built the cathedral of Milan. On the west side of the forecourt is the Farmacia, where the liqueur was distilled, on the north side the Foresteria, or Pilgrims' Lodge, and on the south side the Palazzo Ducale, added in the seventeenth century to house important visitors to the monastery. The church was begun in Gothic but the black and white marble façade is Lombard Renaissance.

The twenty-four cells round the cloisters are really tiny independent houses where the monks lived their separate lives, meeting only three times a day for offices in the church. Each monk had a bedroom and a study with a woodshed and workroom below. Outside each house is a little garden in which the monks grew flowers and sweet herbs. The entrance to each cell is fitted with a turnstile on which the vegetarian meals of the monks were left by the lay brothers who acted as cooks. A rule of silence was observed, relaxed only during a weekly walk last-ing two or three hours. The original order of monks left the Certosa in 1881, and it is now occupied by another monastic order.

Pavia is built on the banks of the river Ticino, which is crossed by an unusual covered bridge. It was the capital of the Lombards from 572 until 774 and the seat of an important university founded in 825. The old ramparts of the city are still partly preserved. Pavia was once called the city of a hundred towers and some of these slender brick structures with their narrow windows are still standing. The church of San Pietro in Ciel d'Oro is of the early 12th century and contains the marble tomb of St. Augustine, erected in 1361. The castle stands in the higher part of the city and was connected to the Certosa by a huge park.

In modern times Pavia is an important industrial centre, particularly famous for the manufacture of sewing machines. The area to the west of the town is a principal rice producing area. Maize, too, is grown to provide the people with one of the staple foods of northern Italy: *polenta*. In Lombardy and the Veneto boiled *polenta* very often takes the place of bread. Most families in northern Italy have a special copper pot for cooking it and a long spoon to stir it with. Once boiled *polenta* can then be fried, grilled or baked, served with different sauces, and as an accompaniment to meat dishes, especially *fegato* (liver) *alla veneziana*.

In Cremona, which is to the east of Pavia, Antonio Stradivari lived and worked, and in the Scuola Internazionale di Liuteria instruments are still made to his ancient formula. He was born in 1644 and died in 1737, and made an average of sixteen violins a year, charging about £4 each for them, a large sum of money in those days. There is an old saying in Cremona: 'As rich as Stradivari', for he was

said to have been very fond of money and very careful with it. All the best violins made by Stradivari have names, such as 'Tuscan', and some are called after famous owners like 'Viotti'. It is still believed that Stradivari had a secret formula, either in the selection of the wood or in the kind of varnish he used.

Cremona's gastronomic speciality is *mostarda*, which is eaten with meat. It is not to be confused with mustard, however, since it consists of glacé fruits in a heavy sweet syrup.

L'utile e il dilettevole

Non tutti i dipendenti della Cossogno passano le vacanze fuori Milano. Aldo Pizzi, un giovane magazziniere che vuole risparmiare per sposarsi presto, si contenta di fare qualche gita nei dintorni, spesso unendo l'utile al dilettevole.

Oggi la meta è la zona di Pavia, e Aldo ha tre passeggeri nella sua vecchia utilitaria: sua madre, che desidera rivedere la Certosa; Gina, la sua fidanzata, che spera di comprare con un forte sconto una macchina da cucire da una sua cugina di Pavia che lavora nella fabbrica; e suo padre, che pensa di spingersi fino alle colline dell'Oltrepo, dove si fa dell'ottimo vino, per comprarne qualche bottiglia.

MADRE Com'è passato in fretta il tempo nella Certosa! È già mezzogiorno.
PADRE Beh, moglie, ora che hai pensato allo spirito, che ne diresti di pensare un po' alla materia?
ALDO Giusto! mi sta venendo un certo appetito . . .
GINA Questi uomini! Non pensano che a mangiare!
P. E a bere.
M. Ma non qui, davanti alla Certosa. Riprendiamo la macchina e fermiamoci in un bel posticino all'ombra . . .

* * *

A. Come mi piace questo polpettone! Mamma, me ne dai un'altra fetta?
M. Ingordo! Te lo sei mangiato quasi tutto! Va là, Gina, dagliene un'altro po'!
P. Aldo, c'è il sale lì vicino a te. Ti dispiace passarmelo?
A. Eccolo.
M. Molto elegante questo tuo vestitino, Gina. Dove l'hai comprato?
A. Macchè comprato, se l'è fatto lei da sola. Tagliato e cucito in due serate.
G. Oh, il modello era molto facile.
M. Chissà cosa sarai capace di fare quando avrai la macchina da cucire nuova.
G. Mia cugina Cesira ha promesso di farmela avere con un buono sconto. A lei la fabbrica la cede a prezzo di costo.
P. Questo vino non mi piace affatto.
A. Sfido io! Comprato al supermarket! Aspetta di essere a Casteggio, dall'Angeloni, e vedrai la differenza.
P. Però lo voglio assaggiare prima di comprarlo.
A. Ma certo, te lo farà assaggiare.
M. Prima passiamo per Pavia, così Gina va dalla Cesira.
G. Veniteci anche voi.
M. No, non è il caso. Noi facciamo un giro per la città.

p. Cioè, per le chiese della città.

m. Ma no, non esageriamo. Mi piacerebbe vedere solo la tomba di Sant'Agostino.

a. E dov'è?

m. In San Pietro in Ciel d'Oro, vicino a Piazza Castello.

p. Allora Gina, puoi trovarci tutti lì in piazza. Mentre la mamma visita San Pietro, noi due potremo vederci comodamente tutto il castello, e magari anche il museo del Risorgimento . . .

Language Practice

1 Gina vorrebbe comprare una macchina da cucire da sua cugina.

  Gina e sua sorella . . .
  . . . sei bottiglie di vino . . .
  . . . dai genitori di Aldo.
  Gina ed io . . .

2 Non ti piace il vino?   Sì, mi piace molto.

  Non vi è piaciuta la Certosa?
  Non ti piace il polpettone?
  Non vi piacerebbe andare a Pavia?
  Non vi è piaciuto San Pietro?
  Non ti piacerebbe vedere il castello?

3 Darai il libro a tuo fratello?   Sì, glielo darò.

  Puoi passare il sale a Gina?   Sì, glielo posso passare./
                              Sì, posso passarglielo.

  Venderai la macchina a tua cugina?
  Aldo ha dato il vino a suo padre?
  Cesira ha mandato il modello a Gina?
  Avete già visitato San Pietro?
  Volete visitare la chiesa?
  Vanno a vedere la tomba di Sant'Agostino?
  Fai assaggiare il caffè al papà?
  Hanno dato il vino alle ragazze?
  Vorresti vedere la Certosa?
  Volevate mandare le cartoline a Aldo?
  Potevamo mangiarci il polpettone?

4 Aldo vuole risparmiare.   Aldo spera di risparmiare.

  Gina desidera comprare una macchina da cucire.
  Sua cugina può fargliela avere con un buono sconto.
  Aldo preferisce fare gite nei dintorni.
  Dobbiamo andare.
  Il signor Pizzi vuole comprare il vino a Casteggio.

Notes

Piacere and *dispiacere*

PIACERE

Piacere has an irregular present tense:

piaccio	piacciamo
piaci	piacete
piace	piacciono

The imperfect and future are regular:

	Imperfect	Future
1st person	piacevo	piacerò
3rd person	piaceva	piacerà

Although *piacere* is used as a translation of 'to like', its real meaning is 'to be pleasing', so, instead of saying: 'I like something', in Italian we say: 'Something is pleasing to me'. Therefore *piacere* is used mostly in the 3rd person, and the subject in English becomes an indirect object in Italian:

Questo vino mi piace or *Mi piace questo vino*
I like this wine (this wine is pleasing to me)
Ci piacerebbe vedere la tomba di Sant'Agostino
We should like to see St. Augustine's tomb
Le piacciono le chiese gotiche
She likes gothic churches

DISPIACERE

The construction and conjugation of *dispiacere* are similar to those of *piacere*, but its meaning is not 'to dislike':

('I dislike this wine' is *Non mi piace questo vino*)

Instead, *dispiacere* has the meaning of 'to be sorry':

Mi dispiace di non poter venire   I'm sorry I can't come

In negative sentences and in questions it also means 'to mind':

Questo vino non mi dispiace   I don't mind this wine
Ti dispiace passarmi il sale?   Would you mind passing me the salt?

Unstressed Particles 4

When a verb has two objects, both of which are particles, the indirect object always precedes the direct object and the final -*i* of the indirect object particle changes to -*e*:

Ti dispiace passarmelo?   Would you mind passing it to me?
Te lo farà assaggiare   He will let you taste it
Se l'è fatto da sola   She made it herself
                             (for herself, by herself)

Both *gli* and *le* become *glie*:

Gina, daglielo tu   Gina, you give it to him!
(This could, of course, also mean: 'Give it to her' or 'Give it to them')

Whenever the verbs: *volere*, *potere*, *dovere* and *sapere* govern an infinitive, the particle or particles may either precede *volere*, *potere* etc., or be joined to the end of the following infinitive:

Me lo puoi passare?	or	*puoi passarmelo?*
Lo voglio assaggiare	or	*voglio assaggiarlo*
Glielo devo dire	or	*devo dirglielo*

However, the particles cannot be joined to the infinitive when it is governed by *fare* and *lasciare*:

Te lo farà assaggiare	He will let you taste it
(not: *farà assaggiartelo*)	
Ha promesso di farmela avere	She has promised to let me have it
Lasciami entrare	Let me come in

Verbs Governing Infinitives

Some verbs do not require any preposition between themselves and the infinitive they govern. They are: *volere*, *desiderare*, *potere*, *dovere*, *fare*, *lasciare*, *preferire* and *sapere* (when it means: 'to know how to do something'):

Aldo vuole risparmiare	Aldo wants to save
Sua madre desidera rivedere la Certosa	His mother wants to see the Certosa again
Posso entrare?	May I come in?
Dobbiamo andare	We must go
Fammi (or *lasciami*) *entrare*	Let me in
Il signor Pizzi preferisce bere il vino di Casteggio	Mr. Pizzi prefers to drink wine from Casteggio
Gina sa cucire a macchina	Gina knows how to use a sewing machine

All other verbs take a preposition before their object infinitive. The most common preposition is *di*, which is used after verbs expressing opinion or intention:

Si contenta di fare gite nei dintorni
He is content to go on trips in the surrounding countryside
Gina spera di comprare una macchina da cucire
Gina hopes to buy a sewing machine
Il signor Pizzi pensa di spingersi fino alle colline dell'Oltrepo Pavese
Mr. Pizzi is thinking of going as far as the hills beyond the river Po (south of Pavia)
Mia cugina ha promesso di farmela avere con un buono sconto
My cousin has promised to let me have it with a good discount
Aspetta di essere a Casteggio
Wait until you get to Casteggio

There are, however, other prepositions used before infinitives. Since it is difficult to give briefly a clear set of rules, we suggest you learn the preposition each verb takes as part of learning how to use the verb. The same verb may, however, take different prepositions, usually with a change of meaning:

Penso di mangiare adesso	I think I'll eat now
Pensa solo a mangiare	All he thinks about is eating

Words ending in *-nte*

Many Italian words ending in *-nte* correspond to English words ending in -nt:

arrogante	arrogant	*indifferente*	indifferent
differente	different	*insignificante*	insignificant
diligente	diligent	*intelligente*	intelligent
distante	distant	*permanente*	permanent
elegante	elegant	*presente*	present
evidente	evident	*protestante*	protestant
frequente	frequent	*residente*	resident
importante	important	*studente*	student

Dipendente (dependent) is used in this context to mean an employee, i.e. a person whose livelihood depends on work given to him.

Text Notes

unendo l'utile al dilettevole – combining business and pleasure
(cf. gerund lesson 7, page 67.)

la meta – destination
In other contexts it can mean 'aim', 'goal'. Do not confuse with *metà* – half.

nella sua vecchia utilitaria – in his old utility car

la Certosa – Carthusian monastery and church

l'Oltrepo (pronounce *Oltrepò*) – the zone beyond the river Po, south of Pavia

beh, moglie – well, wife
This is a teasing way of addressing one's wife.

che ne diresti di pensare
(Cf. lesson 2, page 24 for *ne*).

non pensano che a mangiare – all they think about is eating
non . . . che is an alternative to *soltanto* or *solamente* – only (cf. English 'nothing but' . . .): *non beve che vino* – he only drinks wine, he drinks nothing but wine, *la mamma non visita che chiese* – Mother only visits churches.

un bel posticino . . . polpettone . . . vestitino
Italian uses many diminutive and augmentative endings to modify the meaning of words. *-ino*, *-ina* are commonly used to express smallness and prettiness: *vestito* – dress, *vestitino* – pretty little dress; *ragazza* – girl, *ragazzina* – little girl; *fanale* (of a car) – headlamp, *fanalino* – side or rear light.

The masculine ending *-one*, on the other hand, indicates increase in size: *ragazzo* – boy, *ragazzone* – big boy; it is often applied to feminine words which then change to masculine: *la polpetta* – meat-ball, *il polpettone* – meat-loaf; *una donna* – a woman, *un donnone* – a big woman.

Since the use of these endings often involves further modifications (e.g. *posto* – place, *posticino* – nice little spot) and anomalies, you are advised to use them only when you are sure they can be applied.

te lo sei mangiato quasi tutto! . . . se l'è fatto lei da sola . . . potremo vederci tutto il castello

The use of reflexive particles in some idioms cannot be satisfactorily explained or rendered in English. Apart from a certain emphasis on the fact that the subject is doing something on his own or for his own pleasure and benefit, there is not much difference between the sentences above and the following: *l'hai mangiato quasi tutto!* – you've eaten nearly all of it by yourself, *l'ha fatto lei da sè* – she made it herself, *potremo vedere tutto il castello* – we'll be able to see all of the castle. (Note, however, the change of auxiliary, from *essere*, in the reflexive idioms, to *avere* in the sentences of the second group.) Other examples of common reflexive idioms: *me ne vado* – I'm going, *se ne stava solo in un angolo* – he was in a corner all by himself.

va là – go on!

macchè comprato
(cf. lesson 5, page 54 for *macchè*.)

sfido io! – I should think not!
This idiom confirms a previous statement, whether negative, as in this case, or affirmative: *com'è buono questo vino! sfido io, è dell'Angeloni!* – how good this wine is! I should think so, it's Angeloni's!

supermarket
Not many Italians use the word *supermercato*.

non è il caso – there is no need, there is no point

Sant'Agostino . . . San Pietro
The adjective *santo,-a* when followed by the name of the saint (1) loses its final vowel before names beginning with a vowel: *Sant'Agostino* – St. Augustine, *Sant'Anna* – St. Anne; (2) is reduced to *San* before names of male saints beginning with a consonant: *San Francesco* – St. Francis, *San Pietro* – St. Peter; (3) remains *Santa* before names of female saints beginning with a consonant: *Santa Caterina* – St. Catherine.

L'utile e il dilettevole *Summary*

Nelle sue gite, Aldo Pizzi cerca di unire l'utile al dilettevole. La settimana scorsa è andato con i genitori e la fidanzata nella zona di Pavia.

La madre, che è molto religiosa, ha visitato le chiese più importanti, come la Certosa di Pavia e San Pietro in Ciel d'Oro.

Il padre ha avuto l'occasione di andare a Casteggio per comprare qualche bottiglia dell'ottimo vino che si produce in quella zona.

Gina, la fidanzata, ha fatto visita a una sua cugina che lavora a Pavia in una fabbrica di macchine da cucire. La cugina le ha promesso di fargliene avere una a prezzo di costo. Aldo e Gina ne sono contenti, perchè vogliono sposarsi presto e cercano di risparmiare.

7 Le Marche

The coastline of Le Marche begins with Gabicce Mare, a seaside town built on a crag overhanging the sea. Farther along the coast is Pesaro, an international seaside resort and, with Ancona, the most important city in the province. It was in Pesaro that Rossini was born, the son of a travelling musician who played at local fairs. The Music School has preserved manuscripts and other mementoes of the composer.

The word Marche, meaning frontier provinces, comes from the Germanic word Mark. The region was originally intended as a barrier which would serve to protect the interior of the Empire from attacks, and the Apennines as they descend towards the sea and the coast, make the area very difficult of access.

Urbino, an inland town near to Pesaro, is built on two hills, and like many of the hill towns of Umbria, it was once a free commune. The Romans called it Urbinum Hortense, the little garden town, and it is still surrounded by its walls. In the 15th century the ruling Montefeltro family made their court in Urbino one of the most brilliant in Italy, attracting many of the most important writers, poets and artists of the day. As a reminder of the time when this little town was a leading centre of culture and the arts stands the Palazzo Ducale, one of the masterpieces of Renaissance architecture. Two very famous men were born in Urbino: Bramante and Raphael. Raphael left there in his early youth, although the house where he was born can still be seen, but only one of his paintings, the Ritratto di Gentildonna, hangs in the Art Gallery of Urbino.

It was Bramante who designed the Basilica and the bronze and marble shrine which contains the Santa Casa in Loreto, a few miles south of Ancona. The Santa Casa is the house of Mary which, according to legend, was brought by angels from Nazareth when Palestine was invaded in the 13th century.

Near Gabicce Mare is the Republic of San Marino, the smallest republic in the world and claiming to be the oldest state in Europe. It originated in a settlement formed round the convent of St. Marinus mentioned in texts as early as 885. The Republic mints its own coins and issues its own stamps, and the medieval aspect of the capital has been preserved.

Rossini was a gourmet as well as a great composer, and there are several dishes in the area which are still cooked to his recipes, such as *cannelloni* and *tournedos alla Rossini*.

Urbino col Palazzo Ducale

Affittiamo una villetta

1 Anticamera
2 Corridoio
3
4 } Camere da letto
5 Bagno
6 Gabinetto
7 Soggiorno
8 Cucina
9 Passavivande
10 Ripostiglio
11 Balcone

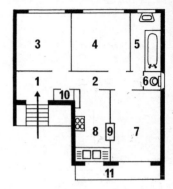

Invece di passare le vacanze in una pensione, quest'anno i Bertelli hanno preso in affitto col figlio una villetta, a Gabicce Mare, vicino a Pesaro.

Bertelli padre, portiere principale dell'officina, è soddisfatto perchè, dividendo l'affitto, la spesa sarà ridotta. Bertelli figlio è contento perchè potrà farsi cucinare dalla moglie ciò che gli piace. Sua moglie, Marcella, pensa che, affidando il bambino alle cure della nonna, potrà andare al mare senza preoccupazioni.

Ecco ora i Bertelli, che vengono condotti alla villetta dall'agente del proprietario.

AGENTE Le darò due chiavi diverse, signor Bertelli. La piccola è per la porta d'ingresso, l'altra per il cancello esterno. Lascino pure le valigie qui in anticamera.

PADRE Va bene. Abbiamo tutto? Giorgio, hai tu la borsa grande?

MADRE No, ce l'ho io. Vado a metterla in cucina.

A. La porta della cucina è la prima a destra nel corridoio.

M. Questa?

A. No, signora: questo è un ripostiglio, dove ci sono i contatori della luce, dell'acqua e del gas. (*They both move into the kitchen.*) Come vede, signora, è una cucina moderna, con acquaio doppio . . .

NUORA Cos'è quello sportello?

A. È il passavivande: comunica con la stanza a fianco, che serve da sala da pranzo e da soggiorno.

P. Giorgio, quale camera da letto prendete voi due?

FIGLIO Sai, Marcella ed io preferiremmo quella vicino al bagno, a causa del bambino.

A. Il bagno è l'ultima stanza a sinistra, in fondo al corridoio.

N. C'è l'acqua calda?

A. Sì, signora, c'è uno scaldabagno a gas.

N. Mi faccia vedere come funziona.

A. È semplice. Venga. Ecco, la leva qui a destra va abbassata per dare il gas, e il bottone al centro va girato per accendere la spia. Quando la spia è accesa, aprendo e chiudendo il rubinetto dell'acqua calda il gas si accende e si spegne automaticamente. C'è altro che vuole sapere?

N. No, grazie.

P. Lei ci ha già dato tutte le informazioni necessarie, mi pare.

A. Allora, se non occorre più nulla . . . buona sera e buone vacanze.

TUTTI Grazie. Buona sera. Arrivederci.

M. Sentite, io devo fare un po' di spesa per la cena. Ho visto diversi negozi all'angolo della strada, e voglio andarci finchè sono ancora aperti.

F. Va bene. Noi cominciamo a disfare le valigie.

M. Marcella, per favore, prendi una pentola e metti su l'acqua per la pasta. Io vado e torno.

Language Practice

1 Quest'anno i Bertelli hanno preso in affitto una villetta perchè così spenderanno di meno.

L'anno prossimo . . .

. . . perchè a Giorgio non piacciono gli alberghi.

. . . non andranno in vacanza . . .

. . . perchè quest'anno hanno speso troppo.

2 Se si gira il bottone, si accende la spia. Girando il bottone, si accende la spia.

Se si apre il rubinetto, il gas si accende.

Se affida il bambino alla nonna, Marcella può andare al mare senza preoccupazioni.

Quando entrate nell'appartamento, lasciate le valigie in anticamera.

Se abbiamo la camera vicino al bagno, vi disturberemo di meno.

Quando l'agente ci ha salutato, ci ha augurato buone vacanze.

3 Quando accendi il gas?   L'ho già acceso.

Quando chiudono il cancello?

Quando compri il biglietto?

Quando decidi?

Quando ti risponderà?

Quando venderete l'appartamento?

Quando vedi Aldo?

Quando prendete il tè?

Quando glielo chiedi?

4 Quante camere da letto ci sono nella villetta?   Ce ne sono due.
  ecc.

Notes

Uses of the Gerund 2

The gerund (*mangiando*, *scrivendo* etc.) is used with the verb *stare* to form the continuous tense (cf. lesson 2 page 23). It is also used by itself to indicate how or why something is done:

Dividendo l'affitto, la spesa sarà ridotta
By sharing the rent expenses will be reduced

Affidando il bambino alle cure della nonna . . .
By entrusting the baby to the grandmother's care . . .
Il gas si accende e si spegne automaticamente aprendo e chiudendo il rubinetto dell'acqua calda
The gas goes on and off automatically by turning on and off the hot water tap

The gerund is invariable, but it is usually fairly obvious from the sense to whom or to what it refers. If in doubt remember that no gerund can refer to the object, so that if both a subject and an object are present in a sentence, the gerund must refer to the subject:

Mario ha visto Giorgio entrando nel caffè
can only mean:
Mario, on entering the coffee bar, saw George
('Mario saw George entering the coffee bar' would be:
Mario ha visto Giorgio che entrava nel caffè.)

Ciò

This pronoun is often used in Italian with the meaning of *questa* or *quella cosa*. When followed by *che* it is translated as 'what':

Ciò è strano	That's strange
Ciò che mi hai detto è strano	What you have told me is strange

Compound Nouns

Some Italian nouns consist of two or more distinct elements combining together to form one word. The most usual combinations are:

Adjective and noun:

il francobollo   postage stamp
(*franco*: free and *bollo*: stamp, i.e. stamp allowing a letter to be delivered free of charge to the addressee.)
la cassaforte   safe
(*cassa*: box and *forte*: strong)

Noun and noun:

il pomodoro   tomato
(*pomo*: apple and *oro*: gold)
la ferrovia   railway
(*ferro*: iron and *via*: way)

Verb and noun:

il passavivande   service hatch
(*passare*: to pass and *vivande*: food)
lo scaldabagno   water heater
(*scaldare*: to heat and *bagno*: bath)

Compound nouns belonging to this last category are usually invariable. All other compound nouns form their plural either by changing only the second half:

francobollo	francobolli
ferrovia	ferrovie

or by changing both:

cass*a*forte   cass*e*fort*i*

Past Participles of Verbs in -*dere*

The past participles of most verbs ending in -*dere* are formed by replacing -*dere*
with -*so*:

decidere	*deciso*	to decide
chiudere	*chiuso*	to shut
perdere	*perso*	to lose

However, if the letter *n* precedes -*dere*, it always disappears:

prendere	*preso*	to take
spendere	*speso*	to spend
accendere	*acceso*	to light

These rules do not apply to the following verbs and their compounds:

cadere	*caduto*	to fall
cedere	*ceduto*	to yield
chiedere	*chiesto*	to ask
credere	*creduto*	to believe
vedere	*veduto/visto*	to see
vendere	*venduto*	to sell
nascondere	*nascosto*	to hide
fondere	*fuso*	to melt
rispondere	*risposto*	to reply

Adverbs in -*mente*

Adverbs can be formed from most adjectives by adding -*mente* to the feminine
singular form:

automatico   automaticamente
semplice   semplicemente

Adjectives ending in -*le* and -*re* drop their final -*e* before adding -*mente*:

facile   facilmente
volgare   volgarmente

The Position of Adjectives

The English word order of qualifying and qualified words as in 'dining-room',
'central knob', 'necessary information' is normally reversed in Italian: *sala da
pranzo, il bottone al centro, le informazioni necessarie.* When the qualifying word is
an adjective the following rules of position apply:

If the quality expressed by an adjective is not an essential or constant characteristic of the noun, the adjective follows the noun:

l'acqua calda
hot water (heat is not a constant feature of water)
la borsa grande
the large bag (as distinct from other smaller bags in the luggage)

If on the other hand the adjective is used to express a quality which is considered as inherent in the noun, then it precedes the noun:

la calda acqua del Mediterraneo

the warm water of the Mediterranean (warmth is its peculiar quality, as opposed to, say, the North Sea)

Note the different meanings of the following adjectives according to their position

Le darò due chiavi diverse	I'll give you two different keys
Ho visto diversi negozi	I saw several shops
una domanda semplice	a simple question (in the sense of an easy question)
una semplice domanda	a simple question (in the sense of a mere question)
un uomo povero	a poor man (i.e. not rich)
un pover'uomo	a poor man, a wretch
Ho comprato un'automobile nuova	I have bought a new (unused) car
Ho comprato una nuova automobile	I have bought a new (different) car

Venire as an Auxiliary Verb

Venire is often used instead of *essere* with a passive construction:

I Bertelli sono condotti alla villa

or:

I Bertelli vengono condotti alla villa

The Bertelli family is taken to the villa

But when a past participle is being used as an adjective you must use *venire* to distinguish between a state and a process:

La porta è chiusa (state)	The door is shut
La porta viene chiusa (process)	The door is being shut (someone is shutting it right now)

Andare as an Auxiliary Verb

Andare followed by a past participle expresses the idea that something must be done:

La leva è abbassata	The lever is in its down position
La leva va abbassata	The lever must be lowered
La lettera era scritta	The letter was already written
La lettera andava scritta	The letter should have been written

The use of *venire* and *andare* in an auxiliary capacity is limited to 'simple' tenses, i.e. those which are not themselves formed by using an auxiliary.

The Plural of the Polite Form of Request

Lascino, the third person plural of the present subjunctive, is an example of the use of the polite form of request in the plural. This form is used only in very formal circumstances, for example in an hotel, or by a waiter in a restaurant. Lecturers or speakers addressing an audience may also use it. The most usual plural of *Lei* is *voi* (cf. lesson 1, page 15).

Text Notes

invece di passare – instead of spending

Note that *invece di*, when followed by a verb, requires the infinitive.

la piccola . . . l'altra – the small one . . . the other one

Note that 'one' is not translated in Italian.

ripostiglio – box-room

This derives from the verb *riporre*, p.p. *riposto* – to put away, to put back in its place.

i contatori – the meters

This word comes from the verb *contare* – to count. Electricity, which is used in Italy mainly for lighting rather than for heating, is commonly called *la luce* – light. In certain parts of Italy water is also metered.

acquaio doppio – double sink

A more technical term for 'sink' is *lavello*: *lavello in acciaio inossidabile* – stainless steel sink.

camera . . . stanza . . . sala

These words often appear to be used indiscriminately (e.g. *stanza*, *sala* or even *camera da bagno*): they have, however, slightly different uses. *Camera* is a private room, the bedroom in particular (*camera da letto*). *Stanza* (from *stare*) is a room in general: *la villetta dei Bertelli ha due camere, ma sei stanze*. *Sala* is either a larger room (*sala da bagno* – fully fitted bathroom) or a room suitable for receiving people (*sala da pranzo* – dining-room).

soggiorno – living-room

This comes from the verb *soggiornare* – to stay, to sojourn.

quella vicino al bagno

It would be just as correct to say *quella vicina al bagno*, changing *vicino* into a feminine adjective agreeing with *camera*.

scaldabagno a gas

The preposition *a* often indicates the way in which machines and appliances function: *pentola a pressione* – pressure cooker, *mulino a vento* – windmill, *stufa a carbone* – coal-burning stove, *ferro a vapore* – steam iron etc.

la spia – the pilot-light

se non occorre più nulla – if you don't need anything . . . (lit. if nothing else is needed)

disfare – to unpack

In other contexts it means 'to undo'. The uses of the prefix *dis-* are similar in Italian and in English: *disaccordo* – disagreement, *disappunto* – disappointment, *disapprovare* – to disapprove, *disarmare* – to disarm, *disintegrare* – to disintegrate, *disordine* – disorder etc. However, many English words beginning with dis- correspond to Italian words beginning with *s-*: disadvantage – *svantaggio*, disconsolate – *sconsolato*, discouraged – *scoraggiato*, etc.

io vado e torno – I'll be back in a minute (lit. I go and come back)

Affittiamo una villetta *Summary*

Quest'anno i Bertelli, padre e figlio, e le loro famiglie, hanno preso in affitto una villetta sulla costa adriatica per spendere di meno e stare più comodi. Vi sono stati condotti dall'agente del proprietario.

La villetta è moderna. La porta d'ingresso si apre nell'anticamera che comunica con il corridoio. Da un lato del corridoio ci sono le due camere da letto, dall'altro la cucina e la stanza di soggiorno che ha un grande balcone. La sala da bagno è in fondo al corridoio. L'agente fa vedere ai Bertelli dove sono i contatori, e come funziona lo scaldabagno a gas.

La villetta piace molto ai Bertelli, che certamente vi passeranno una bella vacanza.

8 Gli Abruzzi

The region of the Abruzzi lies on the borders between central and southern Italy. Most of the area is covered with high mountains, Monte Corno in the Gran Sasso range reaching a height of almost nine thousand five hundred feet. It is essentially a poor district with few industries apart from wool, which is woven mainly for home consumption. In the villages and in centres such as Aquila and Gessopalena women make lace, embroider shawls and weave carpets. Fishing is the main source of wealth of the coastal area where Pescara is the chief port. Grain, vines and olives are grown in the lowlands but on the whole agriculture does not thrive in the Abruzzi. The people have built their homes on the edge of the highest upland plain in their search for a grassy clearing to provide pasture for their flocks and herds, or a piece of land, however infertile, to cultivate. In the more remote parts there are towns and villages which have lived in isolation for centuries.

Although the shepherds and country people greet each other with: *Dio sia lodato* – 'Praise be to God', pagan traces remain in many of the customs and ceremonies of the Abruzzi. At Bisenti, which is said to have been the birthplace of Pontius Pilate, a donkey wreathed in garlands is paraded in a procession headed by a band and accompanied by young girls who carry baskets of grain on their heads. An interesting local festival takes place on the first Thursday in May, St. Dominic's Day, in the village of Cocullo, when the statue of the saint is carried through the streets draped in live snakes. St. Dominic is honoured in this strange way because he is said to have removed the poison from the snakes in the region.

Many other strange customs and beliefs persist in the isolated villages of the Abruzzi. Ghosts, for example, are kept away by placing an axe and a knife on the window-sills, and hail is warded off by making the sign of the cross three times with a scythe in the direction of the threatening clouds.

It is still possible to see the traditional local costume worn on special occasions such as feast days, weddings and christenings. The cap worn by the women of Scanno was specially designed to support the copper pitcher in which they carried water from the well.

Some famous Italians were born in the Abruzzi: Gabriele d'Annunzio was born in Pescara and the philosopher Benedetto Croce in Pescasséroli.

The food of the Abruzzi is simple and the use of local hams, cheese and garlic sausages give it a country flavour. The local way of making *pasta* is called *alla chitarra*, the 'guitar' being the wooden board with wire strings on which the *pasta* is cut. The sauce for *pasta alla chitarra* is usually olive oil and red pepper, a favourite vegetable in this region.

The chief attraction of the Abruzzi is in the mountain areas with their immense plateaux and dense forests. There are many holiday and winter sports resorts, particularly on the plateaux most easily reached from Rome and Naples. The wildest part of the region is now a National Park and here many animals, including chamois and the last few bears of the Apennines are free to roam in their natural surroundings, unpursued by man.

Proprio un vero orso

Gustavo Jannelli, che lavora all'ufficio spedizioni, si lamenta di avere un impiego troppo sedentario. Per compenso, quando è in vacanza a Pescassèroli, fa lunghe gite a piedi in compagnia del fratello maggiore, che è una delle guardie del Parco Nazionale d'Abruzzo.

Il parco si estende lungo l'alta valle del fiume Sangro, tra montagne e foreste, per un'estensione di circa trecento chilometri quadrati; possiede una ricca fauna che comprende dei camosci, e un'ottantina d'esemplari di una rara specie d'orso.

GUSTAVO JANNELLI Nando, aspetta un'attimo . . .

FERDINANDO JANNELLI Sei stanco?

G. Neanche per sogno. Solo che quassù comincia a far fresco e voglio infilarmi il maglione.

F. Buona idea, me lo metto anch'io. Più in là, sotto gli alberi, farà ancora più fresco.

G. Quanto ci vorrà ancora di qui alla cresta?

F. Di questo passo, meno di una ventina di minuti. Ce la fai a tenermi dietro?

G. Sì. Sono meno allenato di te, è vero, ma ce la faccio lo stesso . . .

(*On top of the ridge*)

G. Che stupendo panorama!

F. Conoscevi già questo posto? Ti ci ho mai portato?

G. No, è la prima volta che ci vengo. Come si chiama la valle qui sotto?

F. La val Fondillo. È una delle più belle del parco nazionale. Vedi il valico lì al centro della valle?

G. Sì, lo vedo.

F. Lo chiamano 'il passeggio dell'orso'.

G. E gli orsi ci passeggiano ancora?

F. No, ora non più. Quei pochi che rimangono scendono a valle solo in casi eccezionali, ad esempio, se non trovano da mangiare altrove.

G. Mi piacerebbe vederne uno!

F. Non è facile . . .

G. Tu hai mai incontrato un orso?

F. Solo una volta. Un giorno avevo dato appuntamento a Ciccio Genzano, un'altra guida, alla fontana di San Michele, una sorgente in mezzo a una faggeta. Ero arrivato con una mezz'ora di anticipo, e così mi ero messo a sonnecchiare dietro un grosso sasso, a una ventina di metri dalla sorgente, per ripararmi dal vento. A un certo momento sento un rumore di passi pesanti, e poi uno sciacquìo, come di uno che beve. 'Sarà Ciccio', penso; così grido: – Ciccio, son qua! – e mi sporgo da dietro il sasso. Invece di Ciccio vedo un orso.

G. Che cosa hai fatto allora?

F. Che c'era da fare? niente. Io ho guardato lui, lui ha guardato me. Poi ha fatto un grugnito, ha scosso la testa e se n'è andato com'era venuto.

G. Insomma, non aveva troppa voglia di fare la tua conoscenza.

F. No: proprio un vero orso!

Language Practice

1 Pattern sentences

Gustavo, quando è in vacanza, fa lunghe gite a piedi col fratello maggiore nel Parco Nazionale d'Abruzzo.

Ferdinando si era messo dietro un grosso sasso per ripararsi dal vento mentre aspettava la guida.

Gustavo si alza, si lava e si veste: prima si mette la camicia e poi i pantaloni, si infila le calze e le scarpe e per ultimo si mette il maglione e la giacca.

2 Carla è più piccola di Piero? No, è più piccolo Piero.

Lo zio è più vecchio della zia?
Questo maglione è più caldo della giacca?
Le camere da letto sono più grandi del soggiorno?
La valigia è più grande delle borse?
Il vino è più forte del vermouth?
Bruno è più intelligente delle sue sorelle?

3 È molto bella. Sì, è la più bella di tutte.

È molto brutto.
È molto ricca.
È molto stupida.
È molto alto.

4 Gustavo aveva già visto il Parco No, non l'aveva ancora visto.
  Nazionale?

Era già stato al 'passeggio dell'orso'?
Eri già stato in montagna?
Avevi già assaggiato questo vino?
Avevate già visitato il museo?
Eravate già stati al mare?

Notes

Unstressed Particles 5

Unstressed particles are often used in Italian in connection with clothes or parts of the body where in English we would use a possessive adjective:

Voglio infilarmi il maglione	I want to put on my sweater
Buona idea, me lo metto anch'io	Good idea, I'll put mine on too
Mettiti la giacca!	Put on your jacket
Maria si è scottato il polso	Mary has burned her wrist

The unstressed particles may be used instead of *a me, a te* etc., after expressions indicating place such as *davanti, dietro, sopra, sotto, in mezzo*:

Non ce la faccio a tenerti dietro I can't keep up with you
(Instead of: *Non ce la faccio a tenere dietro a te*)

Mi si è seduta davanti	She sat down in front of me
(Instead of: *Si è seduta davanti a me*)	
Ci è caduto dietro	It fell behind us
(Instead of: *È caduto dietro a noi*).	

Comparisons 1

The adverbs *più* (more) and *meno* (less) are used to make comparisons:

Farà ancora più fresco	It will be even cooler
Ora mi sento meno stanco	I feel less tired now

'Than' is normally translated by *di*:

Meno di una ventina di minuti	Less than twenty minutes or so
Sono meno allenato di te	I am less fit than you
Oggi fa più caldo di ieri	Today it's hotter than yesterday

Che is used, however, between words or expressions belonging to the same grammatical category (i.e. between two adjectives, two nouns, two expressions of time or place etc.):

Questo libro è più divertente che interessante
This book is more amusing than interesting
Carlo ha più dischi che libri
Carla has more records than books
D'estate fa meno caldo in montagna che in pianura
In summer it's less hot in the mountains than in the plain

Il più corresponds to 'the most' or to the ending '-est', *il meno* to 'the least':

È la più bella valle del parco nazionale
It's the most beautiful valley in the national park
Questo libro è il meno interessante di tutti quelli che ho letto
This book is the least interesting of all those I have read
Questi tre quadri sono i più belli del museo
These three pictures are the most beautiful in the museum

A few Italian adjectives already imply the idea of 'more' or 'less' and cannot therefore be preceded by the words *più* or *meno*. One of these is *maggiore* 'greater, elder, larger' and its opposite *minore* 'smaller, younger, shorter':

il suo fratello maggiore
his elder brother
Oggi abbiamo coperto una distanza minore
Today we have covered a shorter distance

The Narrative Present

The present tense is often used in narrations about past happenings to give greater immediacy and vividness to the story. An example of this can be found in the last few sentences of Ferdinando's story about the bear.

The Pluperfect

This tense is formed by the imperfect of the appropriate auxiliary (*essere* or *avere*) and the past participle of the verb. It is used to indicate something which happened even further back in time than the main event, which is already in the past:

Quando sono andato in Abruzzo non avevo ancora visto un orso
Before (lit. when) I went to Abruzzo I hadn't seen a bear
Un giorno avevo dato appuntamento a Ciccio . . .
One day I had arranged to meet Ciccio . . .
Ero arrivato con una mezz'ora di anticipo
I had arrived half an hour early
Mi ero messo a sonnecchiare
I had started to take a nap

Note that even though part of Ferdinando's story is told in the narrative present, he still uses the pluperfect to explain what had happened before he met the bear.

Numerals

The ending *-ina* replacing the last vowel of the tens, from 10 to 90, indicates that the count is only approximate. Note that *dieci* loses its first *i* and becomes *decina*. The resulting numeral is normally preceded by the indefinite article:

una ventina di minuti	about twenty minutes
C'erano solo una trentina di persone	There were only thirty people or so

The corresponding expressions for 'about one hundred', 'about one thousand' are:

un centinaio	pl. *centinaia*
un migliaio	pl. *migliaia*

Ci sono un centinaio di camosci
There are about a hundred chamois
Diverse migliaia di turisti visitano ogni anno il parco nazionale
Several thousand tourists visit the National Park every year

Note that *centinaia* and *migliaia* are feminine.

Text Notes

Jannelli
The letter *j* is sometimes used in old texts and in a few surnames. It should always be pronounced as *i*.

per compenso – to make up for it

una delle guardie del Parco Nazionale d'Abruzzo – one of the guards of the Abruzzo National Park
Certain words, like *guardia* – guard, *spia* – spy, *guida* – guide are always feminine even when they are used to refer to men.

a piedi – on foot

l'alta valle del fiume Sangro – the upper valley of the river Sangro

trecento chilometri quadrati
About 110 square miles

neanche per sogno – not a bit of it

più in là – further on (time or place)

quanto ci vorrà? – how long will it take?
   Ci vuole is an impersonal phrase meaning 'it is necessary' (cf. lesson 9, page 85 and lesson 5 page 55).

ce la fai? – can you manage?
   Here are a few more idiomatic expressions with *la*:
   Finiscila! or *Smettila!* – Stop it!
   Ce l'ha messa tutta – He put everything he had into it
   Non te la prendere – Don't get upset
   Non me la fai – You won't catch me out/take me in

ti ci ho mai portato? – did I ever bring you here?
   Portare does not only mean 'to carry' as in: *il facchino porta le valigie* – the porter carries the luggage, but also 'to bring': *portami qui la valigia* – bring me the suitcase, and 'to take': *ho portato la valigia al deposito bagagli* – I took the case to the left luggage office; *ho portato mio figlio al cinema* – I took my son to the cinema.
   Note that *prendere* also means 'to take', but only in the sense of taking *from* a place: *andrò a prenderlo alla stazione* – I'll go and fetch him from the station (meet him at the station).

il passeggio dell'orso – the Bear's Walk

scendono a valle – they come down to the valley

faggeta – beech wood
   Similarly, *pineta* – pine wood, *querceta* – oak wood, but *oliveto* – olive grove, *aranceto* – orange grove, *roseto* – rose garden.

con una mezz'ora di anticipo – half an hour early

sonnecchiare – to doze

come di uno che beve – as of someone drinking

io ho guardato lui, lui ha guardato me
   (cf. personal pronouns lessons 2 and 4, pages 26 and 45).

proprio un vero orso
   This expression is used in Italian to refer to a person who is unsociable.

Proprio un vero orso *Summary*

Gustavo Jannelli va a passare le vacanze in Abruzzo dal fratello Ferdinando che è una delle guardie del parco nazionale.
   Gustavo, che ha un impiego sedentario all'ufficio spedizioni, non è così allenato come il fratello, ma ce la fa benissimo a seguirlo in lunghe gite a piedi.
   Durante una di queste passeggiate, Ferdinando gli racconta la storia del suo incontro con un orso, uno dei pochi esemplari di una rara specie che vive nelle montagne del parco. A Gustavo piacerebbe assai vederne uno, ma è una cosa molto difficile: gli orsi non sono animali molto socievoli.

Siena, Palio

9 La Puglia

Apulia, or Puglia as it is called, is the part of Italy which is nearest to the Orient. Only forty-four miles of sea separate Cape Otranto from the Albanian coast. In the time of the Roman Empire and the Crusades it was the natural bridge between East and West. Great plains cover most of the area. The Tavoliere di Puglia stretches from the foot of the Gargano mountains in the north as far as Otranto where the Murge Hills begin. Most of the Tavoliere is under wheat. The plains of Bari and Salento have expanses of almond and olive trees and low vineyards laid out in neat geometrical rows.

In the area between Bari, Brindisi and Taranto strange little cone-shaped houses called *trulli* are found. In Alberobello a large part of the town, the Rione Monti, is composed entirely of them and there is a church built in the same style.

Some of the *trulli* are still inhabited, others have been deserted or are occupied only at harvest time. They are of ancient origin and it is uncertain what people first built them, why they took this very distinctive form and why they should have been built only in this area. They are sometimes associated with the *nuraghi* of Sardinia, and sometimes with the 'brochs' or wheelhouses found in the Hebrides and Orkneys.

The walls of the *trulli* are built of slabs of local stone, set without mortar, and they have an inner and an outer layer giving them a total thickness of up to five feet. The roof is built into the shape of a cupola by narrowing layers of stone. Often on top of this cupola a decorative finial is placed, which is sometimes surmounted by a ball or other object. Occasionally the top of the *trullo* is squared off to form a drying area for fruit and vegetables, with a flight of steps leading up to it. On the roofs of some of the *trulli* signs have been painted which are sometimes biblical, sometimes pagan in origin.

Since the walls are very thick, the temperature inside the *trulli* remains constant throughout the year, cooler than the outside temperature in summer and warmer in winter. The rooms are simple, often with wall alcoves where beds are placed or where cooking is done. There is usually only one small window, and the ceiling is high and domed. Two-storey *trulli* are very rare.

Puglia produces a large quantity of olives, most of which are used for making oil, the basis of Italian cooking in general but especially so in the south where no family, however poor, will be without it. Olives which are destined to be table olives must be specially treated, since when fresh and unprocessed they are inedible because of extreme bitterness. At the harvest they are shaken from the trees and then gathered up by hand. They are then left in vats to soak in a dilute alkali such as sodium hydroxide or a salt application to counteract the bitterness.

Puglia has a long coastline bordering the Adriatic and the Ionian Seas. There are many grottoes and caves, the most famous being those of Castellana, the largest in Italy.

According to tradition, the remains of St. Nicholas, who was bishop of Mira and died in 326, were brought to Bari in 1087. The festival to commemorate this event takes place in Bari between the 7th and 10th of May. First there is a procession in costume, then the statue of the saint is carried to the port and set on an altar which is supported by two fishing boats. The altar is taken out to sea, followed by hundreds of craft and anchor is cast at a short distance from the port. There the statue remains for the rest of the day to be visited by thousands of pilgrims.

Un campagnolo di cattivo carattere

I nonni di Luisa Marzullo dirigono una prospera azienda agricola in Puglia, in collaborazione col figlio, commerciante ortofrutticolo, che ne piazza i prodotti sul mercato di Milano.

A Luisa piace la vecchia masseria dei nonni, anche se non può andarci così spesso come loro vorrebbero. È situata non molto lontano da Manfredonia. In un raggio di pochi chilometri si possono raggiungere a sud-est la spiaggia di Siponto ornata da una striscia di pini, a nord le ombrose foreste del Gargano, a sud la vasta pianura del Tavoliere, ricoperta di grano.

LUISA MARZULLO Come va il raccolto quest'anno?

SALVATORE MARZULLO Eh, non così bene come l'anno passato. C'è stata troppa siccità.

L. Eppure papà mi dice che farete più grano di prima.

S. Sì, va bene, perchè abbiamo comprato altri dieci ettari verso il Candelaro, che danno circa 160 quintali; ma la resa per ettaro è più o meno la stessa.

L. E le mandorle?

S. Faremo sì e no venti quintali. Questa non è terra adatta ai mandorli; bisogna andare più giù, dalle parti di Bari.

L. Insomma, voi agricoltori siete sempre pessimisti.

S. Non è questione di essere pessimisti. Realisti, piuttosto. Il fatto è che non si può mai essere sicuri. Ci sono annate migliori e annate peggiori, e solo il Padreterno sa quello che ci manda.

L. Almeno non dirai che le olive vanno male: quelle nere che la nonna ha messo in tavola erano stupende. Non ne ho mai mangiate di così buone.

S. Che vuoi, sono pochi alberi, e per la nostra tavola Concetta prende quelle più grosse. La qualità è buona, ma bisognerebbe produrne di più.

L. Le ha messe in conserva la nonna?

S. Eh sì. Tutto quello che si mangia qui lo ha preparato lei. La roba comprata, oggi è una porcheria. E poi, le olive nere, non c'è nessuno che le sa fare come lei.

CONCETTA MARZULLO (*coming in through the door and overhearing the last words*) Che cosa nessuno sa fare come me?

L. Le olive nere, nonna. Il nonno stava dicendo che sei un'ottima massaia.

C. San Michele Arcangelo, domani viene a piovere! Questo lo dice a te, figlia mia, ma a me non me ne passa una, non me ne passa. Le olive sono troppo amare, o troppo salate; il pane è troppo poco cotto; la minestra gliela faceva meglio sua madre anima benedetta; questo non va bene, quell'altro va male . . .

S. Non dire sciocchezze, che non è vero. Quando fai le cose bene non ti dico mai niente . . .

C. Appunto: dovresti dirmi che le faccio bene. Invece non mi dai mai soddisfazione. Bisogna proprio che venga Luisa da Milano per sentirti parlare bene di me.

L. Insomma, nonno, tu saresti proprio uno di quei campagnoli di cattivo carattere, che pensano sempre al peggio e non sono mai contenti.

S. Giusto; ma come dice tua nonna, farmi cambiare di carattere è semplice: basta che tu venga a trovarci più spesso.

Alberobello, trulli

Language Practice

1 Pattern sentence

Quest'anno il raccolto non è andato bene come l'anno passato perchè c'è stata troppa siccità.

2 Il nonno dice che le olive nessuno le prepara come sua moglie.

. . . la minestra . . .

. . . come vuole lui.

. . . Luisa la prepara . . .

I nonni . . .

3 L'azienda è prospera. Cosa ti pare?   Mi pare che sia prospera.

La nonna fa bene le olive. Cosa ti sembra?

I prodotti sono buoni. Cosa vi sembra?

La resa è la stessa. Cosa ti pare?

Hanno molti mandorli. Cosa vi pare?

Questa roba va comprata. Cosa ti pare?

4 Luisa, devi scrivere la lettera.   Luisa, bisogna che tu scriva la lettera.

Anna, devi venire più spesso.

Bambini, dovete venire subito.

Carlo, devi mandare la valigia domani.

Nonna, devi preparare le olive.

Michele, devi andar via.

Zii, dovete venire lunedì.

Nando, devi parlare con la guida.

Nonni, dovete aspettare fino alle 11.

Notes

Comparisons 2

The following expression is also used in comparisons:

(così) . . . come (così may be omitted)

Non ho mai mangiato olive (così) buone come le tue

I have never eaten olives as good as yours

Non può andarci così spesso come loro vorrebbero

She can't go there as often as they would like

Il raccolto non va così bene come l'anno passato

The crop is not as good as last year's

COMPARATIVES

Two more comparatives of the same type as *maggiore* and *minore* (cf. lesson 8, page 77) are:

migliore (better) and *peggiore* (worse):

Ci sono annate migliori e annate peggiori

There are good years and bad years (lit: there are better and worse years)

Le mandorle di Bari sono di migliore qualità

Bari almonds are of a better quality

Oggi il tempo è peggiore di ieri
Today's weather is worse than yesterday's

Meglio and *peggio* are related to the above comparatives, but are invariable:

Per l'insalata è meglio usare l'olio d'oliva
It's better to use olive oil for salads
Oggi mi sento peggio
Today I'm feeling worse

They can also be used as nouns but only in the singular:

Un ottimista è chi pensa sempre al meglio, mentre un pessimista è chi pensa sempre al peggio
An optimist is someone who always hopes for the best, a pessimist is someone who always thinks the worst

SUPERLATIVES

The words *ottimista* and *pessimista* lead us to two superlatives: *ottimo* and *pessimo*:

Sei un'ottima massaia	You're an excellent housewife
Questa minestra è pessima	This soup is disgusting

As these adjectives already imply the highest degree of goodness or badness, they cannot be preceded by such adverbs as *molto, assai* – 'very', *estremamente* – 'extremely', *infinitamente* – 'infinitely' etc., used in other cases to express superlative quality:

Sono assai stanco
I'm very tired
I nonni sono estremamente contenti di vedere Luisa
Her grandparents are extremely happy to see Luisa

The most common way of forming the superlative, however, is to replace the ending of the adjective with *-issimo, -issima* etc.:

Sono stanchissimo
I nonni sono contentissimi di vedere Luisa

Impersonal phrases

These are formed by some verbs that normally only have an impersonal subject, such as 'it', and are therefore mostly used in the 3rd person:

basta	it's enough
conviene	it's better, it's an advantage
sembra	it seems
pare	it appears

and by a few verbs which only exist in the 3rd person:

bisogna	it's necessary
occorre	it's needed

A further series of impersonal phrases is formed by the verb *essere* in the 3rd person followed by an adjective or a noun:

è bene/male	it's good/bad
è facile/difficile	it's easy/difficult
è tempo/ora	it's time
non è questione	it's not a question

Other tenses may be used besides the present, but always in the 3rd person singular.

These expressions are followed by the infinitive (often preceded by *di*) if no specific reference is made to any individual person or thing:

Per dimagrire basta mangiare di meno
To slim it's enough to eat less
Conviene imparare le lingue straniere
It's an advantage to learn foreign languages
Faceva tanto caldo che sembrava/pareva di essere in un forno
It was so hot that it was like being in an oven
Bisogna andare a Bari per trovare buone mandorle
One must go to Bari to find good almonds
Non occorre alzarsi troppo presto
It's not necessary to get up too early

If, however, reference is made to a person or thing, this subject must be introduced by *che* and the following verb must be in the subjunctive:

Per dimagrire basta che tu mangi di meno
To lose weight, you only have to eat less
Conviene che voi impariate le lingue straniere
It would be to your advantage to learn foreign languages
Sembra che Mario sia stanco
It seems that Mario is tired
Bisogna che i nonni vadano a Bari
The grandparents must go to Bari
Non occorre che tu ti alzi troppo presto
You need not get up too early.

In the following examples the two constructions are compared side by side:

È bene passare le vacanze in famiglia	*È bene che tu passi le vacanze in famiglia*
It's a good thing to spend one's holidays with the family	It's a good thing for you to spend your holidays with the family
È ora di andare a letto	*È ora che Luisa vada a letto*
It's time to go to bed	It's time for Luisa to go to bed
Non è questione di essere pessimisti	*Non è questione che io sia pessimista*
It's not a question of being pessimistic	It's not that I am pessimistic

Reported Speech

Reported speech is normally introduced in Italian by *che*. The verb is in the indicative:

Papà mi dice che farete più grano di prima
Father tells me that you will produce more wheat than before
Dovresti dirmi che faccio le cose bene
You should tell me that I do things well

More examples will be found in later lessons.

The Agreement of the Past Participle after Unstressed Particles

Whenever a tense formed with the auxiliary *avere* is preceded by one of the unstressed particles *lo*, *la*, *li*, *le* or *ne*, the past participle always agrees with the particle. *Lo* and *la* normally drop their vowel before all forms of *avere* and other verbs beginning with a vowel:

Chi ha bevuto il vino?	*L'ho bevuto io*
Who has drunk the wine?	I have drunk it
Chi ha mangiato le olive?	*Le ha mangiate Luisa*
Who has eaten the olives?	Luisa has
Chi ha fatto la minestra?	*L'ha fatta la nonna*
Who has made the soup?	Granny has
Quante olive hai mangiato?	*Ne ho mangiate dieci*
How many olives have you eaten?	I have eaten ten
Chi ha messo in conserva le olive?	*Le ha messe in conserva la nonna*
Who has pickled the olives?	Granny has

Text Notes

azienda agricola – farm

commerciante ortofrutticolo – market gardener

che ne piazza i prodotti sul mercato di Milano – who sells the produce wholesale on the Milan market

si possono raggiungere . . .
   This construction has a passive meaning ('. . . can be reached') and the verb agrees with the 'object'. Compare: *si vedeva una barca sul lago* – a boat could be seen on the lake, and: *si vedevano diverse barche sul lago* – several boats could be seen on the lake.

dieci ettari
   About 25 acres

che ci danno circa 160 quintali – which give us about 160 quintals
   Un quintale is 100 kilograms (220·46 lb.); *quintale* is also used metaphorically as 'ton' is in English: *questa borsa pesa un quintale* – this bag weighs a ton.

Candelaro
   Name of a river.

le mandorle . . . i mandorli
   Names of fruit trees are generally masculine; those of their fruits, feminine:

il melo	*la mela*	apple
il pero	*la pera*	pear
il ciliegio	*la ciliegia*	cherry
il pesco	*la pesca*	peach
il castagno	*la castagna*	chestnut
il mandorlo	*la mandorla*	almond

There are a few exceptions: *il limone* and *il fico* are used for both the fruit and the tree; *l'arancio* is often used to mean the fruit as well as the tree.

più o meno, sì e no – more or less

più giù, dalle parti di Bari – further south, around Bari

non si può mai essere sicuri – one can never be sure

The adjective *sicuri* is plural because after the impersonal *si* (cf. lesson 2, page 25) it could not refer to any specific singular subject, cf. also: *si deve essere contenti di quello che il cielo ci manda* – we must be satisfied with what Heaven sends us.

il Padreterno – God

This name comprises *padre* – father + *eterno* – everlasting. A rather familiar name, often used in proverbial expressions, seldom in a religious context.

mettere in tavola – to serve for lunch/dinner

Note the idiomatic use of the preposition *in*: *è in tavola!* – lunch/dinner is ready!

non ne ho mai mangiate di così buone – I have never eaten such good ones

le olive nere, non c'è nessuno che le sa fare come lei – Black olives, there's no-one who knows how to prepare them as she does

When the object (in this case *le olive nere*) precedes the verb, it must be confirmed by the appropriate unstressed particle (in this case *le*).

San Michele Arcangelo

He is frequently invoked in the region, because of the famous sanctuary dedicated to him at Monte Sant'Angelo, ten miles north of Manfredonia.

domani viene a piovere! – tomorrow the rain will come

Expression of surprise: 'the Heavens are about to fall', 'wonders will never cease'

non me ne passa una, non me ne passa! – nothing escapes him, he doesn't let me get away with anything

The repetition of the verb for emphasis is a characteristic of popular speech.

la minestra gliela faceva meglio sua madre, anima benedetta! – the soup was better when his mother used to make it, bless her soul! (lit. his mother, bless her soul, used to make him better soup!)

The object is placed at the beginning of the sentence for greater emphasis.

non dire sciocchezze, che non è vero! – don't talk nonsense, because it isn't true!

Un campagnolo di cattivo carattere *Summary*

La signorina Luisa, come aveva promesso, è andata in Puglia dai nonni. Essi abitano in una vecchia masseria, a poca distanza da Manfredonia, nella pianura a sud del Gargano. Sono proprietari di un'azienda agricola che produce principalmente grano ed altri cereali, ma anche olive e mandorle. L'azienda è prospera e i suoi prodotti si vendono bene sul mercato di Milano.

Ma il nonno pensa sempre al peggio: dice sempre che il raccolto di quest'anno non è così buono come quello dell'anno passato, che questo non va bene, che quell'altro va male . . . Però basta una visita della nipote per farlo contento e metterlo di buon umore.

10 La Liguria

Monterosso

Monterosso is one of five little towns which together make up the area known as the Cinque Terre. The main characteristic of this part of the Ligurian Coast is the sheerness of the cliffs which drop down to the sea in an almost perpendicular line, rarely leaving room for beach and sand.

Liguria stretches from Ventimiglia to La Spezia and is a long narrow strip of land separated from the plains of northern Italy by the Apennines. The high mountain peaks are very close to the coast. Wedged as it is between mountain and sea, Liguria is the smallest region in Italy and is essentially a region of sailors. Since most of the area is rocky, the people have had to hew enormous steps out of the mountain slopes and transport soil in order to plant olives and vines. The grapes of the Cinque Terre become very sweet because of the sea air and the heat reflected from the rocks, and the wine which they make is very strong and very good.

The Ligurian coast has many very well known seaside resorts, like San Remo and Portofino, some of them as popular in winter as they are in summer on account of the mildness of their climate. Flowers grown here are exported all over the world, and their cultivation has become an industry almost as important to the district as the tourist trade.

The five towns forming the Cinque Terre are Riomaggiore, Manarola, Corniglia, Vernazza and Monterosso. Here the cliffs fall sharply away to the sea and the towns, which are mostly built around bays, seem to cling to the rocky slopes which rise steeply behind them. Monterosso alone of the five towns has a beach, but from each of them there are splendid views along the coast. Because of the rocky nature of the region and the consequent difficulty in reaching it by road, it has remained more isolated and primitive than the rest of the province and each of the little towns has managed to retain its own individuality.

Monterosso is built on a bay and has a ruined castle standing on a small promontory. The hills behind it rise to heights of two to three thousand feet and steep paths pass through vineyards and orchards.

Vernazza is built round a small cove and its parish church rises sheer out of the sea. From Riomaggiore a narrow path hewn out of the rock and bearing the poetic name of Via dell'Amore leads to Manarola.

These little towns look to the sea rather than the land and it is the sea that brings them their livelihood. The houses are tall and narrow. The town centre is the *ciazza* where the fishing nets are hung, where the day's catch is brought and where the fishing boats are repaired. The railway line keeps to the coast, passing through a series of tunnels, but the main road branches inland and by-passes the Cinque Terre. Only in fairly recent years have secondary roads been constructed, making the area accessible from La Spezia.

Genoa is the chief port, not only of Liguria but also of Italy. It is built in a semi-circle round the bay and rises in a series of terraces on the steep hills behind. Centuries ago it was an important and influential sea-republic like Venice, its great rival, and Pisa. One of the many sailors born in Genoa, but undoubtedly the most famous, is Christopher Columbus. The house where he was born, and where he lived as the son of a weaver, has been preserved.

The Banco di San Giorgio in Genoa is said to be the oldest bank in the world. The people of Genoa have a reputation among Italians for being very thrifty and careful with their money.

Genoese cooking has a great deal of originality. Olive oil is used in preference to butter which is more expensive. The *pesto* is a typical dish. Many Genoese kitchens have the special white marble mortar in which the garlic, basil, pine kernels and grated cheese are mixed and bound with olive oil to make a thick sauce for macaroni or minestrone. In Genoa an old saying goes 'Once a foreigner has tasted the *pesto* he never leaves Genoa again'.

Una prenotazione sbagliata

Giorgio Miraglia è stato da poco assunto dal dottor Giudice, che voleva nel suo ufficio commerciale un giovane con una buona conoscenza del francese e dell'inglese. Per le stesse ragioni Giorgio è stato invitato dalla sorella maggiore e dal cognato a passare le vacanze nel loro piccolo albergo a Monterosso. C'è sempre tanto bisogno in un albergo di un interprete per rispondere alle lettere in lingua straniera, e poi ricevere chi le ha scritte. Ma naturalmente non tutti i clienti che Giorgio riceve vengono dall'estero.

MARINA Che cosa dice allora la lettera di quel francese?
GIORGIO Dice che vuol venire con la famiglia, moglie e due figli, per una settimana.

M. Quando?

G. Dal 25 al 31 agosto.

M. Vediamo un po'. Quelli della 12 e della 13 partono il 24 . . . Sì, rispondigli che possiamo riservargli due camere contigue a due letti.

G. C'è poi la lettera della comitiva di Liverpool.

M. Che cosa dicono?

G. Avvertono che arriveranno col treno delle 19,45 invece che con quello delle 16,43.

M. Bisognerà dire a Pèrego di andare a prendere i bagagli alla stazione col furgoncino.

G. Mi pare che ci sia qualcuno all'ingresso. Vado a vedere . . . (*he goes out into the hall*) Buongiorno, signora, desidera?

SIGNORA BELARDI Buongiorno. Ho prenotato una camera per due settimane, col nome Belardi.

G. Belardi . . . Belardi . . . Mi dispiace signora, le troveremo certo una camera, ma la sua prenotazione non mi risulta.

B. Com'è possibile? Ho scritto io stessa che sarei arrivata oggi, e ho qui la vostra cartolina di conferma.

G. Attenda un minuto, che chiamo la proprietaria. Marina, ricordi la lettera di prenotazione della signora Belardi?

M. Buongiorno, signora. Mi ricordo certamente della sua lettera: eccola qui. 'La prego di prenotarmi una camera, con vista sul mare, per quindici giorni, a partire da sabato 28 luglio.'

G. Un momento. Oggi è sabato, ma il 28 luglio è domani!

B. Che sciocca! mi sono sbagliata. Io intendevo prenotare la camera da sabato . . .

M. . . . e noi invece gliel'abbiamo prenotata dal 28 luglio, cioè domani. Ma niente di male. Vediamo subito di sistemare le cose. Giorgio, che camera avevamo dato alla signora?

G. La 5, che è già libera.

M. Come vede, signora, tutto si aggiusta.

B. Meno male! . . . Molte grazie, e mi scusi per l'errore.

M. Si figuri. Può capitare a tutti. Speriamo che Lei trovi la camera di suo gradimento. Ha molti bagagli?

B. No, soltanto questa valigia.

G. Se permette, signora. Mi dia la valigia, così l'accompagno in camera.

B. È molto in alto?

G. No, soltanto al primo piano. Ma la vista, vedrà, è bellissima. Dal balcone si ha un panorama non solo sulla spiaggia, ma anche verso le Cinque Terre.

Language Practice

1 Pattern sentence

Giorgio è stato invitato dalla sorella maggiore e dal cognato a passare le vacanze nel loro piccolo albergo a Monterosso.

2 Dice che vuole una camera a due letti dal 15 luglio al 15 agosto.

... ha prenotato ...
... dal 20 settembre al 5 ottobre.
... due camere con vista sul mare ...
... prenderà ...

3 Hai già prenotato la camera?   Sì, l'ho prenotata ieri.

Hai già scritto la lettera di prenotazione?
Il facchino ha portato i bagagli alla stazione?
Avete già visto la spiaggia?
Hanno ricevuto le cartoline?
Hai comprato i francobolli?

4 Quante camere hai prenotato?   Ne ho prenotate 2.

Quante cartoline hai comprato?
Quanti caffè avete bevuto?
Quante valigie hanno portato?
Quanti ospiti avete avuto?
Quante chiavi ti ha dato?
Quanti libri gli hai venduto?
Quante chiese le hai fatto vedere?
Quante lettere gli hai scritto?

Notes

Reported Speech 2

Whenever verbs of 'saying' (*dire* – to say, *rispondere* – to answer, *avvertire* – to advise, to warn etc.) introduce reported speech, they are constructed with *che* followed by a verb in the indicative or in the conditional.

If the verb of 'saying' is in the present, there is not much difference between Italian and English:

Dice che vuol venire con la famiglia

He says he wants to come with his family

Dice che vorrebbe venire con la famiglia

He says he would like to come with his family

The same applies to sentences where the verb of 'saying' is in the perfect and the other verb in the future:

L'albergo ha risposto che mi riserverà una camera

The hotel has replied that they will reserve me a room

There are, however, differences in the use of the conditional in reported speech. Italian, unlike English, mostly uses the past conditional.

L'albergo ha risposto che mi avrebbe riservato una camera
The hotel replied that they would reserve me a room
Ho scritto che sarei arrivata oggi
I wrote to you that I would arrive today

Whenever verbs of 'saying' introduce statements conveying, not information, but instructions or commands, they are constructed with *di* and the infinitive. Compare:

Gli ho detto che mi accompagnerà in Italia
I told him that he will be coming with me to Italy
and
Gli ho detto di accompagnarmi in Italia
I told him to come with me to Italy

Also:

Rispondigli che possiamo riservargli due camere
Reply that we can reserve two rooms for him
and
Rispondigli di riservarci due camere
Tell him in your reply to reserve two rooms for us

Verbs having the basic meaning of 'to order, to command, to beg, to ask' (such as *ordinare, comandare, pregare, chiedere* etc.) must be constructed with *di* followed by the infinitive, if the person who is given the order is mentioned:

La prego di prenotarmi una camera
I should be grateful if you would book me a room
Ho chiesto al facchino di portarci le valigie in camera
I have asked the porter to bring the luggage to our room.

Otherwise they are constructed with *che* and the subjunctive:

Ho chiesto che ci portino le valigie in camera
I have asked for our luggage to be brought to the room

Expressions of Opinion

Verbs of opinion (*mi pare, mi sembra* – it seems to me, *penso, credo* – I think, I believe etc.) are constructed:
with *di* followed by the infinitive, if the subject of both verbs is the same:

Mi pare di perdere tempo	It seems to me I'm wasting time
Mario crede di avere la febbre	Mario thinks he's got a temperature

with *che* followed by the subjunctive, if the subject of the second verb is different:

Mi pare che voi perdiate tempo	It seems to me you're wasting time
Mario crede che io abbia la febbre	Mario thinks I've got a temperature

Different functions of *che*

Note the different functions (and meanings) of *che* in the following examples:
WHO

Giorgio è stato assunto dal dottor Giudice che voleva un giovane con una buona conoscenza delle lingue
Giorgio has been given a job by Dr. Giudice, who was looking for a young man with a good knowledge of foreign languages

WHOM

Non tutti i clienti che Giorgio riceve vengono dall'estero

Not all the clients whom Giorgio receives come from abroad

WHICH

Abbiamo dato alla signora la camera 5, che è già libera

We have given Mrs. Belardi room no. 5, which is already free

WHAT . . . ?

Che camera avevamo dato alla signora?

What room did we book for Mrs. Belardi?

Che (cosa) dice quella lettera?

What does that letter say?

WHAT A . . .

Che sciocca!

What a fool I am!

THAT

Dicono che arriveranno col treno

They say (that) they are arriving by train

WHILE

Attenda un minuto che chiamo la proprietaria

Wait a minute while I call the owner

Adjectives in *-bile*

Many Italian adjectives ending in *-bile* correspond to English adjectives ending in -ble. Here are a few examples:

abile	able
accessibile	accessible
compatibile	compatible
incompatibile	incompatible
inestimabile	inestimable
inevitabile	inevitable
infallibile	infallible
insolubile	insoluble
insuperabile	insuperable
impossibile	impossible
possibile	possible
probabile	probable

Note that *sensibile* means 'sensitive' or 'notable':

una pelle sensibile	a sensitive skin
un sensibile aumento dei prezzi	a notable increase in prices

Text Notes

è stato assunto dal dottor Giudice

Assunto is the past participle of the verb *assumere* – to employ. *Da* ('by') introduces the agent in this and in the following sentence: *è stato invitato dalla sorella maggiore* – he has been invited by his elder sister.

in lingua straniera – in foreign languages

Note that *straniero* always means 'foreigner', whereas *forestiero* which also means 'foreigner' can sometimes be used to mean 'stranger' i.e. not belonging to a particular place or community.

poi ricevere chi le ha scritte – and then to receive the people who have written them

(cf. *chi* lesson 1, page 16.)

l'estero – foreign countries, abroad

As a noun it is always singular, but it can also be an adjective: *tabacchi nazionali ed esteri* – home-grown and imported tobacco (on sale here).

della 12 e della 13

Camera is understood.

due camere contigue – two adjoining rooms

a due letti – with single beds

When booking rooms in Italian hotels, married couples should specify whether they want *letto matrimoniale* – a double bed (usually larger than its English counterpart), or *letti gemelli* – twin beds.

la comitiva di Liverpool – the party from Liverpool

il treno delle 19,45

Ore is understood. Note that decimal figures are always preceded by a comma, and not by a decimal point.

col nome Belardi – in the name of Belardi

la sua prenotazione non mi risulta – I don't seem to have your booking

Risultare means 'to appear', 'to turn out to be . . .': *non mi risulta che sia arrivata* – as far as I know she hasn't arrived, *la firma è risultata falsa* – the signature turned out to be a forgery, *ho viaggiato tutta la notte e ne risulta che sono stanco* – I have been travelling all night and as a result I'm tired.

la vostra cartolina di conferma – your (card in) confirmation

ricordi la lettera? or *ti ricordi della lettera?* – do you remember the letter?

The two constructions are virtually interchangeable: *ricordare qualche cosa* – to remember something, *ricordare qualche cosa a qualcuno* – to remind someone of something, *ricordarsi di qualche cosa* – to remind oneself of (i.e. to remember) something.

niente di male – there's no problem, there's no harm done

vediamo subito di sistemare le cose – let's see how things can be arranged

si figuri – don't mention it

An idiom with several meanings: *si figuri com'ero contenta di essere in Italia* – just imagine how happy I was to be in Italy, *posso prenderti una sigaretta? figurati!* – may I take one of your cigarettes? by all means!

di suo gradimento – to your liking

Una prenotazione sbagliata *Summary*

Giorgio Miraglia, che ha una buona conoscenza del francese e dell'inglese, è andato a passare le vacanze a Monterosso, nell'albergo della sorella e del cognato. Così li ha aiutati a ricevere i turisti stranieri e a rispondere alle loro lettere. Ma spesso Giorgio riceve anche clienti italiani, come la signora Belardi, che ha prenotato una camera a partire dall'ultimo sabato di luglio. C'è stato però un errore. Nella sua lettera la signora aveva indicato la data della domenica, e così la sua prenotazione non risultava nel registro.

Ma niente di male: le cose si sono sistemate subito. La camera riservata alla signora Belardi era già libera. È una bella camera, al primo piano, con vista sul mare, che certo la signora troverà di suo gradimento.

11 La Toscana

Tirrenia is one of the many seaside resorts along the Tuscan coast and has a wide beach bordered by thick pinewoods. The Tuscan coast is varied, with straight stretches of sandy beach alternating with shores broken by rocky coves and cliffs. Inland the landscape is hilly and the soil fertile. A characteristic sight is the team of white oxen used for work in the fields. Artistically Tuscany is perhaps the most important region in Italy, having not only Florence but also Pisa, Siena and Lucca within its borders.

Lucca was important in Roman times and had an amphitheatre of considerable size. It was a republic in the 12th and 13th centuries and in 1805 Napoleon made his brother-in-law Prince of Lucca. Several of the churches date back to the 12th and 13th centuries and some of the houses are of the late Middle Ages. The streets are narrow and without pavements. Lucca is an important centre of the olive oil industry and is surrounded by rich agricultural land.

Pisa lies ten miles to the south-west of Lucca in a flat and almost treeless plain. It was originally a Greek colony, then an Etruscan and later a Roman town. The Romans used the mouth of the river as a naval base. At the beginning of the 11th century Pisa became a powerful sea republic and established centres for trade in Palermo and Calabria. The wealth obtained through these trading activities was used to finance the building of churches and monuments in the town. The most famous part of Pisa is to the north-west where the Cathedral, the Baptistry, the Leaning Tower and the Campo Santo are to be found. The Campo Santo was designed at the end of the 13th century to hold sacred earth brought back in ship-loads from Palestine. The Cathedral, entirely of marble, was begun in 1064 and consecrated at the end of the following century. The cost of building was met by booty from six Saracen ships. The circular Baptistry with its dome of white marble was built in the 12th century and has a pulpit sculpted by Niccolò Pisano.

The Palio which is held at Siena twice a year, on July 2nd and on August 15th, is one of the most colourful festivals in Italy. At all other times Siena is quiet and peaceful, but during Palio time the streets are full of people, confusion and noise and the festivities continue far into the night. For the occasion the main square is transformed into an arena and seats are arranged in tiers along the sides. The Palio was originally a cloak of velvet or brocade but for the festival it has become a silk banner showing the image of the Virgin. The climax of the festival is the competition for the Palio in which the various districts of Siena take part. Each district chooses a horse and a jockey to represent them, and lots are drawn to decide which of the districts may compete in the actual race. Various processions in costume take place and each horse is ceremoniously conducted by pages and standard bearers in medieval costume to the local parish church for a special benediction. Before the race can begin, the *carroccio* which was captured from the Florentines and is a symbol of the victory which the festival celebrates, is drawn round the Piazza by the traditional white oxen. The race itself lasts only a very short time, but the excitement of the people is at fever pitch. The jockeys ride bareback and wear protective clothing which they well need since no rules of fair play operate during the race; indeed one of the chief aims seems to be to obstruct as many of the other competitors as possible.

Tuscany is the home of Italy's most famous wine: *chianti*. The name *chianti* is protected by law, and only wine produced from grapes grown in the area between Florence and Siena can be called *chianti classico*.

Correndo sull'autostrada

Agostino e Silvana Biraghi si sono conosciuti in fabbrica d'estate, e si sono sposati otto mesi dopo, prima di Pasqua. Hanno fatto solo un brevissimo viaggio di nozze a Firenze, tra il venerdì santo e il lunedì dell'Angelo, per poter conservare intatta la loro quindicina di ferie estive. Le passano in agosto, campeggiando nella pineta di Tirrenia, circa quindici chilometri a sud di Pisa.

Ascoltiamoli mentre, nel tardo pomeriggio, corrono in macchina sull'autostrada Firenze-mare.

SILVANA Arriveremo prima che faccia buio? È bene piantar la tenda quando c'è ancora luce.

AGOSTINO Ma certo. Abbiamo appena passato Lucca, tra un quarto d'ora saremo alla fine dell'autostrada.

S. Se non incontriamo troppo traffico dalle parti di Pisa, tra un'oretta siamo arrivati.

A. Beh, anche se è un po' più di un'ora, con la nostra macchinetta non conviene andar più svelti di così.

S. Oh, sai, andiamo di buon passo. Ci abbiamo messo sette ore da Milano, non contando le soste per il pranzo e per cambiar la gomma. Mica male, no?

A. A proposito, bisognerà far riparare la gomma al primo garage dopo l'autostrada.

S. Basta che tu la dia a riparare domani mattina . . .

A. Mettiamo che se ne fori un'altra: come faremo senza una ruota di ricambio?

S. Ma no, non succederà niente. Tiriamo avanti fino a Tirrenia.

A. Ora l'aria si è un po' rinfrescata, ma che caldo che ha fatto tutto il giorno! Se continua così . . .

S. Comunque non si dovrebbe star male al campeggio. È in pineta, all'ombra . . .

A. Ombra d'accordo, ma speriamo che sia anche un po' ventilato.

S. Se avremo troppo caldo ci tufferemo in acqua: il mare è a due passi.

A. Di giorno, va bene. Ma se non c'è aria, io non riesco a dormire, e non potremo mica passar la notte in acqua!

S. Tutta la notte certo no. Ma un bagno, prima di addormentarci . . .

A. Un bagno? Che idee!

S. E perché no? L'acqua è ancora calda, sulla spiaggia non c'è nessuno. Si sta benissimo, te lo dico io.

A. E tu come fai a saperlo?

S. Io? Io ho già fatto dei bagni di notte.

A. Ah! A poco a poco saltano fuori i segreti del tuo passato!

S. Ma che segreti d'Egitto! Te l'avrò raccontato almeno cento volte che mia sorella ed io abbiamo fatto un bagno a mezzanotte, quando siamo andate in Riviera due anni fa.

A. Davvero? Io non ricordo . . .

S. Già, tu non stai mai a sentire quando io ti racconto le cose.

A. Però . . . in fondo non è mica una cattiva idea . . .

S. Vedrai! È molto romantico, la spiaggia silenziosa, il mare luccicante sotto la luna piena . . .

A. Mi dispiace deluderti, ma questa notte la luna è al primo quarto.

S. E che importa? Meglio una nuotata sotto un quarto di luna che una doccia nei lavatoi sotto una lampadina elettrica!

Language Practice

1 Pattern sentence

Agostino e Silvana Biraghi si sono conosciuti in fabbrica d'estate e si sono sposati otto mesi dopo.

2 Mi può riparare la gomma per le 2? perchè devo arrivare a Tirrenia prima che faccia buio.
. . . cambiare la ruota . . .
. . . per le 6,30 . . .
. . . perchè vorrei essere al campeggio . . .

3 Quando arrivo, ti telefono.   Se arrivo stasera, ti telefono.

Quando finisco il libro, te lo dò.
Quando lo vedo, ti avverto.
Quando parto, ti lascio la macchina.
Quando compro il vino, te ne dò una bottiglia.
Quando vengo da te, ti faccio vedere le fotografie.

4 Questo vestito è molto bello.   Questo vestito è bellissimo.

Questa lezione è molto facile.
Questo vino è molto buono.
Questo sole è molto caldo.
Questa signora è molto elegante.
Questi esercizi sono molto difficili.

5 Quando parte per Londra?   Non so, ma spero di vederlo prima
                                                            che parta.

Quando va a Roma?
Quando torna a Milano?
Quando lascia l'albergo?
Quando prende le ferie estive?

Notes

Prima di ... Prima che ...

Compare the following uses of *prima*:

Ci arriveremo prima	We'll get there earlier
Ci arriveremo prima di notte	We'll get there before nightfall
Faremo il bagno prima di andare a dormire	We'll have a swim before going to bed
Arriveremo prima che faccia buio	We'll get there before it gets dark

Prima di is always followed by a noun, a personal pronoun or a name, or by an infinitive. *Prima che* is followed by a verb in the subjunctive.

Conditional sentences 1: Present and Future

These are sentences describing what happens or will happen if certain conditions are fulfilled. Examples:

Se non c'è aria, io non riesco a dormire
If it's stuffy (if there is no air), I can't sleep

Se non incontriamo troppo traffico, tra un'oretta siamo arrivati
If we don't meet too much traffic, we'll be there in about an hour

The previous sentence could also have both verbs in the future indicative.

Se non incontreremo troppo traffico, tra un'oretta saremo arrivati

[Note, incidentally, that sentences with two futures also occur after *quando*:

Quando arriverò, ti scriverò or *Quando sarò arrivato, ti scriverò*
I'll write to you when I get there]

For conditional sentences in the past, cf. lesson 12.

Superlatives in *-issimo, -issima* etc.

Here are a few more examples of the superlative of adjectives formed by adding the ending *-issimo* (cf. lesson 9, page 85):

Hanno fatto solo un brevissimo viaggio di nozze
They went on only a very short honeymoon

La giornata è stata caldissima
The day was very hot

The superlative of adverbs not ending in *-mente* (like *bene* – well, *male* – ill or badly, *presto* – soon, *tardi* – late etc.) also ends in *-issimo* but is invariable:

Si sta benissimo, te lo dico io	It's fine there, I can assure you
Arriveremo tardissimo	We'll arrive very late

Adverbs in *-mente* derived from adjectives, form their superlative by adding *-mente* to the superlative of the feminine adjective:

lento	*lentissimo*	*lentamente*	*lentissimamente*

This form, however, is rarely used and *molto lentamente* is preferable:

Camminava molto lentamente   He was walking very slowly

Text Notes

si sono conosciuti in fabbrica – they met in the factory

The 1st, 2nd and 3rd person plural reflexive particles often have a 'reciprocal' meaning ('each other'): *scriviamoci regolarmente* – let's write to each other regularly, *si davano del tu* – they addressed each other with 'tu'.

Conoscere una persona means 'to meet' or 'to be acquainted with a person', and in this sense may often be translated as 'to know': *conosci Giorgio?* – do you know Giorgio? (cf. lesson 4, page 46). In a different context, *conoscere* means 'to have full knowledge or experience of': *conosce bene la letteratura italiana* – he knows Italian literature well, *conosce la vita* – he knows life. In this respect it differs from *sapere*, which means 'to know specific facts or items of information, to know how to': *sai in che anno morì Dante?* – do you know the year of Dante's death?, *non so nuotare* – I don't know how to swim, *mia moglie non sa parlare italiano* – my wife does not speak Italian.

d'estate

The preposition *di* is often used with words indicating parts of the year or the day, seasons etc., not qualified by any adjective: *d'estate andiamo al mare, d'inverno andiamo a sciare in montagna* – in the summer we go to the seaside, in winter we go skiing in the mountains, *ho già fatto dei bagni di notte* – I have gone swimming at night before.

If these words are qualified, then they are preceded by the definite article without any preposition, or by the prepositional article *nel, nello* etc.: *l'estate del 1967 siamo andati in Italia* – we went to Italy in the summer of 1967, *nel tardo pomeriggio* – late in the afternoon, *la mattina presto* – early in the morning etc.

viaggio di nozze – honeymoon (lit. marriage journey)

Honeymoon is often literally translated into Italian as *luna di miele*.

venerdì santo

All days in *la settimana santa* – Holy Week, are distinguished by the adjective *santo*, not only Good Friday.

lunedì dell'Angelo – Easter Monday

It is also called *la Pasquetta* in some parts of Italy. Note incidentally that the names of months and days of the week are normally written in Italian without capitals.

ferie (f. pl., no sing.) – holidays

Ferragosto (= *ferie d'agosto*) – August Bank Holiday (August 15th in Italy). Note, however, that *giorni feriali* means weekdays or working days (this apparent anomaly derives from the ecclesiastical calendar where 'ferial days' are the weekdays when the feasts of patron saints may be celebrated, as opposed to Sunday, the Lord's Day).

correre in macchina – to drive

dalle parti di Pisa – around Pisa

non conviene andar più svelti di così
Remember that the adjective is always plural after impersonal expressions (cf. lesson 10, page 87).

di buon passo – at a good pace

ci abbiamo messo
(cf. lesson 3, page 37).

mica male, no? – not bad at all, is it?
Mica, the original meaning of which is 'bread-crumb', is one of those words indicating small quantities which are used in various languages to reinforce the negative (cf. English: 'not a bit', French: 'ne . . . pas' or 'ne . . . point'). It normally comes after *non* followed by a verb, as in these examples: *non potremo mica passare la notte in acqua?* – we can't possibly spend the night in the sea, *in fondo non è mica una cattiva idea* – on the whole it's not a bad idea at all.

bisognerà far riparare la gomma – we must have the tyre mended
Note the use of *fare* followed by another verb in the sense of 'to have something done': the person who is asked to do it is the indirect object, or occasionally the agent: *ho fatto piantar la tenda a mio marito* – I asked my husband to put up the tent, *fagli vedere come si pianta la tenda* – show him how to put up the tent, *bisognerà far riparare la macchina dal meccanico* – we must have the car repaired by the engineer.

mettiamo che . . . – let's suppose that . . .

tiriamo avanti – let's go on

io non riesco a dormire – I shan't be able to sleep
The verb *riuscire* has an irregular conjugation in the present:

Indicative		Subjunctive	
riesco	riusciamo	riesca	riusciamo
riesci	riuscite	riesca	riusciate
riesce	riescono	riesca	riescano

It means 'to succeed' in doing something, 'to manage', and is frequently found as the translation of 'can'. Note, however, that 'can/could' is often used in English to express three different concepts, requiring different translations in Italian:

I can't swim (I don't know how to)	*Non so nuotare*
I can't swim (because of some physical disability)	*Non posso nuotare*
I can't swim (said usually when one is trying and not succeeding perhaps because of adverse external conditions)	*Non riesco a nuotare*

bagno
This is used in Italian to mean both a bath and a swim in the sea (*bagno di mare*). Notice that Italians say *fare un bagno* – to have a bath, to take a swim.

te lo dico io – I assure you, I'm telling you

come fai a saperlo? – how do you know?

Other uses of *fare a* + infinitive: *come fai a vederci in questo buio?* – how do you manage to see in such darkness?, *non capisco come fanno a non piacervi gli spaghetti* – I don't understand how you fail to like spaghetti.

ma che segreti d'Egitto! – what secrets are you talking about?

D'Egitto – of or from Egypt. This is used to express strong denial, often in conjunction with *ma che* (or *macchè*, cf. lesson 5, page 54). The nearest English equivalent of this idiom is 'my foot': 'secrets my foot!'

almeno cento volte – at least a hundred times

Note *una volta* – once, *due volte* – twice, *tre volte* – three times etc.

luccicante

Many words ending in *-ante* and *-ente* (cf. lesson 6, page 62), are directly connected with verbs, e.g. *protestante* with *protestare* –to protest, *luccicante* with *luccicare* – to glitter, to shine, *conveniente* with the impersonal form *conviene* – it's useful, expedient etc. In this case they are called the 'present participle' of the verb, and are the Italian equivalent of English participles in -ing used as adjectives: *l'orologio parlante* – the speaking clock, *vino spumante* – sparkling (lit. frothing) wine, *una notizia sorprendente* – a surprising item of news, *acqua bollente* – boiling water etc.

sotto un quarto di luna

The phases of the moon in Italian are: *luna nuova* – new moon, *primo quarto* – first quarter, *luna piena* – full moon, *ultimo quarto* – last or third quarter. Other words connected with the moon are: *mezzaluna* – half moon, *luna crescente* – waxing moon, *luna calante* – waning moon; note also: *sotto la luna* – in the moonlight, *sotto il sole* – in the sun, *sotto la pioggia* – in the rain, *sotto la neve* – in the snow.

Correndo sull'autostrada Summary

Agostino e Silvana Biraghi sono due giovani sposi che non hanno fatto il tradizionale viaggio di nozze per poter conservare intatta la loro quindicina di ferie estive. Hanno deciso di prenderle in agosto, campeggiando nella pineta di Tirrenia, sulla costa a sud di Pisa. Hanno fatto il viaggio in macchina, quasi sempre sull'autostrada, in poco più di otto ore, fermandosi solo per il pranzo e per cambiare una gomma.

Agostino spera che a Tirrenia non farà così caldo come durante il viaggio. Silvana vuole fare un bagno di notte, per rinfrescarsi prima di andare a dormire sotto la tenda: l'idea sembra un po' strana ad Agostino. Ma poi l'accetta. Peccato solo che la luna sia al primo quarto: con la luna piena sarebbe molto più romantico!

12 La Sardegna

Sardegna, nuraghe

Sardinia is the second largest of the Mediterranean islands. Politically it forms part of Italy, but has remained less populated, and more simple and antiquated in its way of life and its customs. The people of Sardinia speak *sardo*, which is not easily understood by Italians. The island has metal and coal mines which provide its two main resources, but principally it is a pastoral land with nearly half the total area under permanent grazing. Many of the people are shepherds, taking their flocks to graze in the silent hills and mountain areas. The characteristic which most distinguishes Sardinia is the great silence and loneliness of the countryside. The principal towns are Cagliari, Nuoro and Sassari, the capitals of the three provinces.

The Costa Smeralda extends for fifty-four kilometres along the Gallura coast and is famous for its hidden coves between giant cliffs of granite. Olbia and Golfo Aranci are two of the principal ports of entry to Sardinia and have lonely beaches with very good sands. La Maddalena is at the centre of an archipelago which includes Caprera, Garibaldi's home for many years. It was off La Maddalena that Nelson had his headquarters during the blockade of the French fleet at Toulon from October 1803 until January 1805. It is possible that he never went ashore to see the little town with its steep, narrow streets curving like bridges over the angle of the hill on which the town is built. A stone causeway, il Ponte della Moneta, links La Maddalena to Caprera, which is now almost entirely uninhabited. It covers an area of about ten square miles and like La Maddalena it was originally occupied by nomadic shepherds moving between Corsica and Sardinia. Since it is formed of granite rock, few crops can be cultivated with any success, and it is, therefore, only used for fishing. Garibaldi first came to Caprera in 1855, buying the northern part of the island for about £360. Later he built his home, La Casa Bianca, a flat-roofed white mansion where many mementoes have been preserved, such as the red shirt he wore during the assault on Sicily. The island, which now belongs to the state, is quiet and peaceful, the only sound being the lapping of the sea against the shore.

One of the greatest charms of the many prehistoric remains to be found in Sardinia is their mystery. In many cases one can only guess at their origin and purpose. The landscape is dotted with thousands of stone towers, called *nuraghi*, and no-one is quite sure just why they were built, or who constructed them. Many theories have been put forward as to their purpose: that they were monumental tombs, that they were trophies of victory, and that they were temples of sacrifice and worship. They belong to the Sardinian Bronze Age civilization, and, since in many cases fortified villages of partially stone-built round huts appear in close proximity to them, it is possible that they may have been used as the residences of chieftains. Usually they are found on isolated heights among the mountains or on artificial mounds in the plains. They are conical in shape and contain two and sometimes three chambers, one above the other and connected by a spiral staircase.

Quell'impiastro di Dino

Cesare Cossogno, nipote del fondatore della ditta, ha ora diciotto anni, ripete la terza classe del liceo scientifico, e con grave disappunto del nonno e del padre non sembra molto attirato nè dagli studi nè dall'industria. Ai motori elettrici preferisce la pesca subacquea, che quest'anno pratica in Sardegna, sulla Costa Smeralda. Eccolo sulla terrazza di un albergo, in vista del golfo di Marinella, che chiacchiera con amici.

GIACOMO Ma come! Poco fa pareva che foste pieni di energie e ora non ce la fate nemmeno a staccarvi dalla poltrona.

FRANCESCA Io sono stanca. Per muovermi fa troppo caldo adesso. Più tardi.

G. Potremmo andare in macchina fino al nuraghe.

CESARE Quale macchina?

G. La tua. La mia purtroppo è in garage e la riavrò domani.

C. Bisognava che ci pensaste prima: l'ho prestata a Dino.

G. Che disastro! e dov'è andato Dino?

C. È andato a Caprera, a vedere la casa di Garibaldi.

F. Caprera? Sapevo che la tua auto era una fuoriserie, Cesare, ma non immaginavo che fosse anche anfibia . . .

C. Spiritosa! Voglio dire, è andato in macchina fino a Palau, e lì prenderà il battello per Caprera.

F. Gliel'hai spiegato bene? Quello lì è capace di non fermarsi al pontile e di proseguire diritto.

C. Va là! D'accordo che Dino è distratto, ma non fino a questo punto.

G. Ah no? Bisognava che tu lo vedessi ieri . . . Già: non ti è venuto nemmeno in mente di chiedermi perchè la mia macchina è in garage. . . .

F. Gliel'ha guastata Dino!

C. Che cos'ha fatto?

G. Oh, niente di grave. Ha solamente scambiato il bocchettone dell'olio per il tappo del radiatore, col risultato che mi ha riempito d'acqua la coppa dell'olio . . .

F. . . . e avrebbe anche messo olio nel radiatore se Giacomo non l'avesse fermato a tempo.

G. Così ho dovuto farla rimorchiare dal meccanico più vicino per farci cambiare l'olio; e il meccanico più vicino è a cinque chilometri.

C. Che impiastro, quel Dino! E io che vado a prestargli la mia macchina!

F. Beh, ormai è fatta. Non ci pensare.

C. Potremmo però chiedere in prestito la camionetta dell'albergo . . .

G. Non è possibile.

C. E perchè?

G. Perchè è partita poco fa per Golfo Aranci, tirandosi dietro a rimorchio la mia macchina.

C. In conclusione oggi non possiamo andare al nuraghe.

G. Ma sì che possiamo andarci!

F. E come?

G. Avete dimenticato che esiste anche un utile mezzo di trasporto chiamato 'gambe'. Prendiamo il treno da Rudalza fino a Olbia e poi facciamo cinque chilometri a piedi.

C. Cinque chilometri a piedi!

F. Senti, Giacomino, perchè tanta fretta? Il nuraghe è lì che aspetta da più di duemila anni. Ci aspetterà ancora per qualche giorno, no?

Language Practice

1 Pattern sentence

Cesare Cossogno, che ha ora diciotto anni, ripete la terza classe del liceo scientifico e non sembra molto attirato nè dagli studi, nè dall'industria.

2 È andato in macchina fino a Venezia e lì prenderà l'aereo per Milano.

Andrò . . .

. . . in treno . . .

. . . il pullman . . .

. . . . in battello . . .

3 Sono le 16. Il treno parte fra 20 minuti.   Allora parte alle 16,20.

Sono le 17,15. Il treno parte fra   7 minuti.
Sono le 10,10. Il treno parte fra   8 minuti.
Sono le   8,35. Il treno parte fra 16 minuti.
Sono le 12,55. Il treno parte fra 10 minuti.
Sono le 11,42. Il treno parte fra 18 minuti.

4 Se arriva domani, lo vedrò.   Se arrivasse domani, lo vedrei.

  Se ho soldi, andrò in Puglia.

  Se ho tempo, gli scrivo stasera.

  Se piove, stiamo a casa.

  Se non viene, gli telefono.

  Se vuoi, posso accompagnarti.

  Se vado a casa, prendo l'ombrello.

  Se mi scrive, gli rispondo subito.

  Se fa bel tempo, andiamo al mare.

  Se il treno parte in orario, arriviamo alle 8.

  Se vieni a casa mia, ti faccio mangiare un risotto alla milanese.

Notes

Conjugation of the Past, Perfect and Pluperfect Subjunctive

PAST SUBJUNCTIVE

This tense is formed by replacing the -re of the infinitive with the following endings:

ENDINGS	-ARE viaggiare	-ERE avere	-IRE partire	essere
-ssi	viaggiassi	avessi	partissi	fossi
-ssi	viaggiassi	avessi	partissi	fossi
-sse	viaggiasse	avesse	partisse	fosse
-ssimo	viaggiassimo	avessimo	partissimo	fossimo
-ste	viaggiaste	aveste	partiste	foste
-ssero	viaggiassero	avessero	partissero	fossero

Fare, bere and *dire* form their past subjunctive from the non-contracted form of the infinitive (cf. lesson 2, page 24): *facessi, bevessi, dicessi* etc. The past subjunctive of *stare* is *stessi*.

PERFECT AND PLUPERFECT SUBJUNCTIVE

These two compound tenses are formed by the present and the past subjunctive respectively of the appropriate auxiliary, and the past participle of the verb:

	PERFECT	PLUPERFECT
essere	sia stato	fossi stato
avere	abbia avuto	avessi avuto
viaggiare	abbia viaggiato	avessi viaggiato
partire	sia partito	fossi partito etc.

Sequence of tenses

We have already seen several sentences composed of two parts joined together by *che*: the first (main clause) having a verb in the present indicative, the second, following *che* (dependent clause), having a verb in the present subjunctive, e.g.

Penso che Mario arrivi oggi   I think Mario may arrive today

There are, of course, several other combinations of tenses in the two clauses, and those in the following tables and examples are the most common:

Main clause	Time of related event in respect of main verb		
	(a) FUTURE	(b) CONTEMPORARY	(c) PAST
1 Present indicative	Future indicative	Present subjunctive	Perfect/past subjunctive
2 Perfect/ imperfect indicative	Conditional (present) past	Past subjunctive	Pluperfect subjunctive
3 Present conditional	Past subjunctive		Pluperfect subjunctive
4 Past conditional	Pluperfect subjunctive		

Examples:

1a   *Mario arriverà domani*
       Mario will arrive tomorrow
1b   *Mario arrivi oggi*
     Penso che   Mario may arrive today
1c   I think that   *adesso Mario sia già arrivato*
       Mario has already arrived by now
       allora Mario fosse già arrivato
       Mario had already arrived by then
2a   *Mario sarebbe arrivato il giorno dopo*
       Mario would arrive the following day
2b   *Ho pensato che/pensavo che*   *Mario stesse arrivando*
    I thought that   Mario was going to come
2c   *Mario fosse già arrivato*
       Mario had already arrived
3ab   *Sarebbe meglio che Mario venisse domani/oggi*
      It would be better if Mario were to come tomorrow/today
3c   *Sarebbe meglio che Mario fosse venuto ieri*
      It would be better if Mario had come yesterday
4   *Sarebbe stato meglio che Mario fosse venuto*
      It would have been better if Mario had come

This fairly detailed table and the related examples are given for reference, but only sequences of the following type will appear in the text:

Pare che siate pieni di energie
It seems that you are full of energy
Poco fa pareva che foste pieni di energie
A few moments ago it looked as if you were full of energy
Bisogna che tu lo veda oggi
You ought to see him today
Bisognava che tu lo vedessi ieri
You ought to have seen him yesterday
Penso che possiamo andarci in macchina
I think we can go there by car
Pensavo che potessimo andarci in macchina
I thought we could go there by car

Conditional sentences

The pattern of conditional sentences having a conditional in the main clause and a subjunctive in the dependent clause is similar to that of sentences 3ab, 3c and 4 in the previous paragraph. These sentences may also be written as follows:

3ab *Sarebbe meglio se Mario venisse domani/oggi*
3c   *Sarebbe meglio se Mario fosse venuto ieri*
4   *Sarebbe stato meglio se Mario fosse venuto*

In most conditional sentences where the main verb is not impersonal, as in the previous examples, the order of the clauses is reversed: the 'if' clause (dependent) normally comes first:

Se non avessimo incontrato troppo traffico, saremmo arrivati dopo un'ora
If we had not met too much traffic, we would have made it in an hour
Se non facesse troppo caldo, potremmo fare una passeggiata
If it were not too hot, we could go for a walk

It may, however, also come after the main clause:

Avrebbe messo olio nel radiatore, se Giacomo non l'avesse fermato a tempo
He would have poured oil into the radiator, if Giacomo had not stopped him in time

Nouns in *-ore* and *-tore*

Some Italian words ending in *-ore* correspond to English nouns (and adjectives) ending in -or/-our. If they are nouns, they are masculine, e.g.:

aggressore	aggressor	*predecessore*	predecessor
autore	author	*professore*	professor
colore	colour	*splendore*	splendour
errore	error	*tenore*	tenor
onore	honour	*terrore*	terror
inferiore	inferior	*vigore*	vigour
oppressore	oppressor		etc.

A sub-category of these words is formed by nouns ending in *-tore*. A few of these have English equivalents in -or:

alligatore	alligator	*impostore*	impostor
commentatore	commentator	*inventore*	inventor
creatore	creator	*motore*	motor, engine
creditore	creditor	*senatore*	senator

Many more, however, do not resemble their English equivalents, but it is not difficult to understand their meaning, since they are usually related to verbs, and in general indicate a person who performs the action expressed by the verb, e.g.:

fondare	to found	*fondatore*	founder
fumare	to smoke	*fumatore*	smoker
narrare	to tell a story	*narratore*	storyteller
remare	to row	*rematore*	oarsman
servire	to serve	*servitore*	servant

Some masculine nouns ending in *-tore* have a feminine form in *-trice*:

attore	actor	*attrice*	actress
autore	author	*autrice*	authoress
imperatore	emperor	*imperatrice*	empress
pittore	painter	*pittrice*	woman painter
scrittore	writer	*scrittrice*	woman writer
			etc.

Text Notes

ripetere la terza classe
After five years of *scuola elementare* (primary school) and three years of *scuola media unica* (lit. unified middle school), forming the compulsory period of education, Italian boys and girls who have passed a special qualifying examination (*diploma di scuola media*), may proceed to several types of secondary schools, including the *liceo classico* and the *liceo scientifico*, roughly corresponding to grammar schools with classical or scientific bias. The state examination at the end of a five-year period of *liceo classico* or of *liceo scientifico*, qualifies for university entry. All pupils who fail to receive pass grades at the end of any one year in any subject must sit for an examination in that subject at a special October session. If they do not pass it, they do another year in the same class.

una fuoriserie – a 'special' (lit. outside the production line)
Strictly speaking this is used of a car with a special engine or with a coach-built body, but often it refers to a car slightly modified and 'personalized' by the addition of various accessories.

spiritosa! – very witty, aren't you!

quello lì (or *quello là*) – that one
Usually this has a slightly derogatory implication.

d'accordo che Dino è distratto – granted that Dino is absent-minded

già, non ti è venuto nemmeno in mente – of course, it didn't even cross your mind

il bocchettone dell'olio – the oil-filler pipe

la coppa dell'olio – the sump

che impiastro! – what a nuisance!
   This is used only to refer to people.

e io che vado a prestargli la mia macchina! – and I go and lend him my car!

chiedere in prestito – to ask for the loan of
   Prendere in prestito – to borrow, *dare in prestito* – to lend.

tirandosi dietro
   (cf. lesson 8, page 77). *Tirando dietro a sè*

ma sì che possiamo andarci! – but of course we can go there!

Quell'impiastro di Dino! *Summary*

Cesare Cossogno, nipote del fondatore della ditta, chiacchiera con due amici, Giacomo e Francesca, sulla terrazza di un albergo in Sardegna.

I tre giovani non sanno bene come passare il pomeriggio. Giacomo propone di andare in macchina a visitare un nuraghe; ma in quale macchina? Francesca non ne ha. Cesare ha prestato la sua a Dino, un altro amico. Quella di Giacomo è guasta, perchè quell'impiastro di Dino, che l'aveva presa in prestito il giorno prima, ha riempito d'acqua la coppa dell'olio invece del radiatore. Resterebbe la camionetta dell'albergo: ma nemmeno quella è disponibile, perchè sta rimorchiando la macchina di Giacomo dal meccanico.

In conclusione, se i tre amici vorranno andare a visitare il nuraghe, dovranno servirsi del treno fino a Olbia, e poi di un mezzo di trasporto molto poco moderno, ma sempre utile: le gambe.

13 La Calabria

Calabria, strada di paese

Much of Calabria is desolate. Parts of it are without roads and some of the villages can only be reached by stony paths. Attempts have been made to develop industry, but raw materials are completely lacking and there are no rivers of any importance. For many years emigration has been thought of as the only answer to the economic problems facing the area. Traditionally this emigration was directed to America, but after the First World War America restricted her quota of immigrants. In modern times many of the southern Italian workers can be absorbed by the new industries in the north of Italy around Milan. Although it has become a movement within the country itself, many of those who move from the south still think of it as 'emigration'.

Overpopulation is a major problem, although this is hard to believe as you drive through the deserted mountains of the Aspromonte, the southernmost range in Italy. Occasionally high up a village or town may appear, miles from anywhere up an unmade road. In ancient times these mountains supplied the Athenians and Sicilians with wood for shipbuilding and they were famous for their cattle. The Sila is a vast plateau at a height of three thousand eight hundred feet. Woods of pine and fir give it an Alpine appearance and the climate is very good, fresher in summer than in the lowlands. The northern part of the Sila is called the Sila Greca and here there are many Albanian villages. The Albanians came to Calabria in the 15th century to escape persecution by the Turks. In the Sila they found mountains and forests similar to those they had left behind them and they founded a group of villages which now have names like Santa Sofia d'Epiro and San Demetrio. The people have retained their own institutions, their dress and their language.

8

San Giovanni in Fiore grew up around the monastery founded in the 11th century by San Gioacchino who, according to legend, was guided to the eastern slope of the Sila by oxen which John the Baptist had revealed to him in a dream.

The province of Calabria is surrounded on three sides by the sea. The Ionian coast is known as the Costa dei Gelsomini because of the many jasmine plantations bordering it.

The most widely used vegetable in Calabria is the aubergine which is the basis of many of the local specialities. Swordfish, caught on the Reggio coast, are grilled, cooked in cutlets or stewed.

Ritorno al paese natio

Pasquale Mancuso, di San Giovanni in Fiore, nella Sila, è partito dal suo paese natio cinque anni fa per cercar fortuna al Nord. Trovato un lavoro, ha fatto venire a Milano tre anni dopo la sorella Filomena.

Ora Pasquale è tornitore alla Cossogno, e Filomena fa la commessa in un grande magazzino della città. Quest'anno, dopo due anni di assenza, messi da parte dei risparmi, hanno deciso di ritornare a casa per le vacanze. Sono soli in uno scompartimento del rapido Napoli – Reggio Calabria, fortunatamente poco affollato.

FILOMENA Aahh . . . Che ora è?

PASQUALE Hai dormito bene? Sono le sei e un quarto.

F. Dove siamo?

P. Abbiamo appena passato Sapri.

F. Guarda Pasquale che vista magnifica. Com'è bello il mare!

P. Questa è la costa di Maratea. La moglie del direttore è venuta proprio da queste parti a passare le vacanze, due anni fa.

F. Beata lei! I milanesi vengono al Sud a divertirsi, e noi andiamo a Milano a lavorare.

P. Che vuoi fare? Bisogna che il turismo si sviluppi per portare il benessere in questa regione.

F. Bisognerebbe che si sviluppassero tante altre cose . . .

P. Hai ragione, ma occorre pure che si cominci da qualche parte. Dietro ai turisti arriva il commercio. Venissero più milanesi a sciare nella Sila! Forse meno sangiovannesi se ne andrebbero a Milano . . .

F. E poi la vita a Milano non è brutta. Ci sono tante cose, il cinema, la televisione, che non esistono ancora nei nostri paesi . . .

CONTROLLORE Buongiorno. Prego, biglietti.

F. Li hai tu i biglietti?

P. Li ho io, nel portafoglio. . . . Ecco . . .

C. Andate a San Giovanni in Fiore? Sapete che dovete cambiare a Paola, e poi a Cosenza.

P. Sì, lo sappiamo. A che ora si arriva a Paola?

C. Alle 7,32. La coincidenza per Cosenza è alle 8,12.

F. Da che binario parte?

C. Questo non lo so. È meglio che domandiate quando arrivate. Buongiorno.

p. Mi sembra che, l'ultima volta che ho fatto questo viaggio, il treno per Cosenza partisse dal binario a fianco.

f. Pasquale, domandiamo lo stesso. Potrebbero avere cambiato. Tanto abbiamo tutto il tempo.

p. A quest'ora dobbiamo essere in Calabria . . .

f. Perchè a quest'ora? E prima dov'eravamo? Maratea non è in Calabria?

p. Maratea è in Basilicata, ignorante! Guarda, ecco la stazione di Praia a Mare . . . Ora siamo in Calabria.

f. Si vede. Guarda che vista . . . e che colori . . . Qui il mare è ancora più bello. . . .

Language Practice

1 Pattern sentence

Pasquale Mancuso, di San Giovanni in Fiore, è partito dal suo paese natio cinque anni fa per cercare fortuna a Milano.

2 Ora Filomena fa la commessa in un grande magazzino della città.

Due anni fa . . .
. . . la segretaria . . .
. . . in un ufficio . . .
. . . di Milano.
Fra un mese . . .

3 Prendiamo i biglietti?   Li ho già presi.

Gli chiediamo il libro?
Facciamo la minestra?
Gli diciamo la risposta?
Compriamo i cerini?
Scriviamo le cartoline?
Portiamo su le valigie?
Rispondiamo a tuo fratello?
Telefoniamo alla mamma?
Facciamo una fotografia a Carla?
Diamo il programma a Cesare?

4 Ci sono andato diversi anni fa.   Ci sono andato qualche anno fa.

Due o tre giorni fa è venuta mia zia.
Sono andati a trovarla due o tre settimane fa.
Diversi mesi fa ho fatto una gita in montagna.
Vengo fra cinque minuti.
Arriverà fra due o tre ore.
Abbiamo fatto diverse belle gite in macchina.

Notes

Past Participle used without an auxiliary

The past participle, as well as being part of the verb, is also an adjective and is often used by itself without an auxiliary.

The past participle of verbs that would take *essere* as their auxiliary agrees with the subject as usual:

> *Venuta a Maratea per passare le vacanze, la moglie del direttore si è divertita molto*
> Having been to Maratea for her holidays, the director's wife enjoyed herself very much
> *Partito dal suo paese, Pasquale Mancuso ha trovato lavoro a Milano*
> Having left his village, Pasquale Mancuso found work in Milan

The past participle of verbs that would take *avere* as their auxiliary agrees with the object:

> *Trovato un lavoro, Filomena si è stabilita a Milano*
> Having found a job, Filomena settled in Milan
> *Messi da parte dei risparmi, Pasquale ha deciso di ritornare a casa per le vacanze*
> Having saved some money, Pasquale decided to return home for the holidays.

Text Notes

paese natio – native village

The adjective *natio* is rarely used in any other context and *natale* or *di nascita* are more common: *città natale* – native town, *luogo di nascita* – birthplace. Note that, in a different context *paese natio* may mean 'native country': *Pasquale è partito dal suo paese natio per cercar fortuna all'estero* – Pasquale left his native country to seek his fortune abroad.

ha fatto venire a Milano la sorella Filomena – he had his sister Filomena come to Milan

Fare followed by an infinitive (cf. lesson 11, page 103) can also mean 'to make something happen': *è ora di far mangiare il bambino* – it's time to feed the baby (lit. to make the baby eat), *lo faccia entrare* – ask him to come in.

è tornitore (or *è un tornitore*) – he is a machine lathe operator; *fa la commessa* – she works as a salesgirl

The expression with *essere* refers to the status or professional qualifications of people; the second, with *fare*, to the work they do, the way they act, or a role they play: *Alessandro Cossogno è il fondatore della ditta* – Alessandro Cossogno is the founder of the firm, *Mario è un ingegnere e fa il disegnatore di moda* – Mario is a graduate in engineering who works as a fashion designer, *non fare lo sciocco* – don't be stupid, *Luisa faceva la seconda strega nel 'Macbeth'* – Luisa played the second witch in 'Macbeth'. When what people are coincides with what they do, the two expressions are interchangeable: *Marisa è un'infermiera* – Marisa is a qualified nurse, *Marisa fa l'infermiera* – Marisa works as a nurse. Note that with *fare* the definite article is used.

un grande magazzino – a department store

della città

Nouns stressed on the last syllable are invariable: *la città, le città*. A number of nouns in *-tà* correspond to English nouns in -ty:

città	city, or town
santità	sanctity or holiness
onestà	honesty
abilità	ability
difficoltà	difficulty
velocità	velocity or speed

del rapido Napoli-Reggio Calabria

Italian trains are classified according to their speed and to the frequency of their intermediate stops:

accelerato: local train, stopping at every station

diretto: faster train, not stopping at every station

direttissimo: fast train, stopping only at the most important stations

rapido: a fast inter-city service (sometimes only first class), for which a supplement (*supplemento rapido*) must be paid

occorre pure che si cominci da qualche parte – it has to start somewhere though

milanesi . . . sangiovannesi

As in English there are no definite rules in Italian for forming the names used to refer to the inhabitants of different towns.

Here are some of the most common:

Torino	torinese	Spoleto	spoletino
Milano	milanese	Aquila	aquilano
Genova	genovese	degli Abruzzi	
Pavia	pavese	Roma	romano
Padova	padovano	Napoli	napoletano
Venezia	veneziano	Bari	barese
Ravenna	ravennate	Messina	messinese
Pisa	pisano	Palermo	palermitano
Firenze	fiorentino	Cagliari	cagliaritano
Siena	senese	Parma	* parmigiano

* (local people maintain that this adjective applies only to cheese and wish to be known as *parmensi*.)

venissero più milanesi a sciare nella Sila! – if only more Milanese would come to ski in the Sila!

The imperfect subjunctive is used in exclamations to express a wish that may not be fulfilled. Note that this and the following sentence could be combined into a conditional without altering the tenses: *se più milanesi venissero a sciare nella Sila, forse meno sangiovannesi se ne andrebbero a Milano* – if only more Milanese came to ski in the Sila, perhaps fewer people from San Giovanni would go away to Milan.

prego, biglietti – tickets, please

Here are some other uses of *prego* (from the verb *pregare* – to pray, to ask):
Molte grazie. Prego, si figuri! – Many thanks. Please don't mention it! *Mi fa vedere l'orario ferroviario? Prego!* – May I see the railway time-table? By all means! *Prego, si accomodi* – Please take a seat.

la coincidenza – the connection (trains, buses etc.)

binario – platform in a railway station (lit. the rails)

ignorante – silly

si vede – that's obvious

Ritorno al paese natio *Summary*

Pasquale Mancuso e la sorella Filomena sono due calabresi che sono andati a Milano per cercar fortuna. La settimana scorsa erano in viaggio per il loro paese natale, che non rivedevano da due anni.

Le lunghe ore di viaggio hanno dato loro l'occasione di riflettere sulla loro situazione. A Filomena sembra strano che i calabresi debbano andare a Milano per lavorare, mentre i milanesi vanno in Calabria a passare le vacanze. Pasquale spera che lo sviluppo dell'industria turistica aiuti un maggior numero di calabresi a trovar lavoro nella propria terra. Fratello e sorella si trovano d'accordo che a Milano ci sono tante cose interessanti, il cinema, la televisione, bei negozi, divertimenti, che aiutano a passare i momenti di libertà e a tollerare meglio la lontananza da casa.

14 Latina

Gaeta

Latina is a small province lying along the coast between Rome and Naples. In spite of the fact that it was founded only as recently as 1934, the area it comprises is one of the oldest inhabited regions in Italy. In one of the caves of Monte Circeo, la Grotta Guattari, remains were found dating back some sixty thousand years. The long domination of near-by Rome has left many remains of temples, amphitheatres, bridges and villas throughout the region.

Some of the towns are new, like Latina, the provincial capital, while others, like Formia and Gaeta have traditions which date back many centuries. Formia was a well-known and popular holiday resort in Roman times and is built on the slopes of the Aurunci hills rising behind it. It is famous for its cooking, particularly for its fish dishes and for its Roman wines: Cecubo, Falernum and Formiano. Gaeta is the legendary burial place of Caieta, nurse of Aeneas. Its port is large and sheltered and opens on to a gulf. Minturno is built on the site of a Roman town whose people fled to the hills to escape malaria and pirate raids. The ruins of the old Roman city can be seen near the present town of Minturno, and in the summer months performances of plays are given in the Roman theatre.

The province of Latina, with its coastline extending for almost a hundred kilometres, was an easy prey to pirates, and the many towers and forts to be seen along the shore of the Tyrrhenian sea were built as a measure of defence.

Sperlonga is rapidly developing into a popular tourist resort. It is a picturesque seaside town built on a rock which descends in an almost perpendicular line to the sea. It has been famous since antiquity for its many caves and grottoes. Once the Emperor Tiberius used to come here, attracted by the silence and peacefulness of the place and the deep blue of the sea. In the neighbourhood there are many remains of the palace of Tiberius and of Roman villas.

Uno studioso del passato

La costa a sud di Roma, specialmente il tratto dal Monte Circeo a Minturno, era altrettanto nota agli antichi quanto lo è ai turisti di oggi. Ezio Bertelli-Giusti, direttore di un noto quotidiano della capitale, lo sta spiegando ad Alessandro Cossogno (padre del Cesare che abbiamo già incontrato) il quale è andato a visitarlo nella sua villa di Sperlonga.

ALESSANDRO COSSOGNO E questa è la villa di uno studioso del passato? A me questo arredamento modernissimo fa piuttosto pensare al futuro!

EZIO BERTELLI-GIUSTI Lascia stare l'interno e vieni al balcone. Pensa alle favole di Omero e di Virgilio connesse al monte Circeo, che era già abitato centomila anni fa! Guarda i monti Ausoni, lì dietro. Il nome non ti dice nulla?

C. Beh . . . a dir la verità . . .

BG. Gli Ausoni, gli antichissimi abitanti della zona. Dal loro nome i poeti latini chiamarono Ausonia l'Italia.

C. Ah sì . . . Ora ricordo. Vecchie memorie di liceo. Ma a me, sai, il latino non andava troppo a genio , . .

BG. Già, tu avevi scelto la scienza fin d'allora. Ricordi almeno il nome della stazione dove sei sceso ieri?

C. Quello sì. Fondi-Sperlonga.

BG. Bene. Fondi era il luogo d'origine del famoso vino Cecubo. Lo imbarcavano per Roma, nel porto di Terracina, là a destra . . .

C. E se lo bevevano gli imperatori!

BG. Spesso venivano a berlo qui. Tiberio ha dato il suo nome ad una delle grotte marine di Sperlonga, quindi forse ci passò una vacanza.

C. Anche gli altri romani antichi ci venivano in villeggiatura?

BG. Pare di sì. Sappiamo che Cicerone aveva una villa nei pressi di Formia, dall'altra parte del promontorio di Gaeta che vedi a sinistra. Fu lì che i sicari di Marco Antonio lo ammazzarono.

C. Il solito destino degli intellettuali che vogliono immischiarsi di politica.

BG. Meglio che se ne occupino gli intellettuali che i generali come Antonio! . . . Insomma, capisci ora perchè questa zona mi fa ritornare nel passato?

C. Quello di ritornare al passato è un vizio tipicamente romano, e qualsiasi pretesto è buono: nostalgia delle antiche glorie . . .

BG. Per me non si tratta di nostalgia, ma di equilibrio. A Roma sono immerso fino al collo nelle attività e nelle ansietà di oggi, e anche nelle previsioni del domani. Qui trovo il necessario compenso nell'immaginare la vita di ieri. È più sereno.

C. Ci vieni spesso?

BG. Ogni estate, almeno dal 1935, quando la casa passò a mio padre. Mio nonno l'acquistò nel '28, ma la lasciò più o meno com'era.

c. Chi l'ha rimodernata?

BG. Mio padre. Sai com'è, prima cominciò col costruire quest'ala, poi finì col rifare la casa di sana pianta.

c. E tu? Qual'è stato il tuo contributo?

BG. Io? Da quel pigro romano passatista che sono, io non ci ho fatto proprio niente.

c. E questo arredamento ultramoderno?

BG. Questo è tutta opera di mia moglie!

Language Practice

1 Pattern sentence.

Alessandro Cossogno è andato a trovare l'amico Ezio Bertelli-Giusti, direttore di un noto quotidiano della capitale.

2 Sappiamo che aveva una villa nei pressi di Sperlonga.

. . . vicino a . . .
. . . ha una fabbrica . . .
. . . abita in un paesino . . .
Penso . . .

3 Andrò domani.   Sono andato ieri.

Verrà la settimana prossima.
Lo vedrò stasera.
Farò un bagno a mezzanotte.
Gli dovrò telefonare fra un'ora.
Le scriveremo una cartolina.

4 Ha fatto caldo ieri.   Farà caldo domani.

È venuto a prendere i libri ieri.
Non hanno potuto venire ieri.
Ieri gli ho chiesto un consiglio.
Sono stato a casa ieri.
Ieri hanno preso il treno per la Calabria.

5 Bisogna che Pasquale prenda il treno delle 6,30.   Bisognava che Pasquale prendesse il treno delle 6,30.

Credo che tu abbia messo da parte dei risparmi.
Penso che Filomena sia partita per cercare fortuna al Nord.
Mi sembra che il treno parta dal binario a fianco.
Non so se si deva cambiare a Cosenza.
Basta che tu chieda al controllore.

Notes

Comparisons 3

The following expressions are also used in comparisons:

tanto ....quanto

altrettanto...............quanto

Examples:

Roma è una città tanto ricca di storia quanto di arte

Rome is a city as rich in history as in art

Ezio si interessa tanto alla storia antica quanto alla vita moderna

Ezio is as interested in ancient history as in modern life

La costa a sud di Roma era altrettanto nota agli antichi quanto lo è ai turisti di oggi

The coast south of Rome was equally well known to the people of ancient times as it is to the tourists of today

When the verb *essere* needs to be repeated, as in the sentence above, one must either repeat the adjective or replace it by the particle *lo* (*quanto è nota ai turisti* or *quanto lo è ai turisti*).

Il quale, la quale, i quali, le quali.

These forms can replace *che*, when *che* refers to people,
either to avoid repetition:

Lo sta spiegando ad Alessandro Cossogno (padre del Cesare che abbiamo già incontrato), il quale è andato a visitarlo

He is explaining it to Alessandro Cossogno (father of Cesare whom we have already met), who has gone to visit him

or ambiguity:
In the following sentence:

Ho conosciuto la moglie del direttore che mi ha parlato bene di te

I met the wife of the director, who spoke very well of you

che may either refer to *la moglie* or to *il direttore*. The use of *il quale* or *la quale* avoids the ambiguity:

Ho conosciuto la moglie del direttore il quale mi ha parlato bene di te

I met the wife of the director who spoke well of you

Ho conosciuto la moglie del direttore la quale mi ha parlato bene di te

I met the director's wife who spoke well of you

This ambiguity is more likely to arise in the written language.

Past Historic of *-are* and *-ire* verbs

The past historic is formed by replacing the *-are* and *-ire* infinitive endings with the following:

		ANDARE	FINIRE
-ai	-ii	andai	finii
-asti	-isti	andasti	finisti
-ò	-ì	andò	finì
-ammo	-immo	andammo	finimmo
-aste	-iste	andaste	finiste
-arono	-irono	andarono	finirono

For *-ere* verbs cf. lesson 15.

This tense describes past happenings (often in a fairly remote past) and is used particularly when one does not want to imply any connection with the present. In this respect it differs from the perfect which always maintains some connection, however vague, with the present, even though it describes a completed event in the past:

> *Tiberio ha dato il suo nome ad una delle grotte marine di Sperlonga, quindi forse ci passò una vacanza*
> Tiberius has given his name to one of the grottoes of Sperlonga, therefore perhaps he spent a holiday there
> *Mio nonno la lasciò più o meno com'era; chi l'ha rimodernata?*
> My grandfather left it more or less as it was; who has modernized it?

The past historic is used more frequently in written than in spoken language. In the spoken language its frequency varies with the region (cf. lesson 15).

Infinitive used as a Noun

The infinitive in Italian is often used as a noun, and is normally translated into English by the '-ing' form of the verb:

> *Questo continuo andare e venire mi disturba*
> This continual coming and going disturbs me
> *Qui trovo il necessario compenso nell'immaginare la vita di ieri*
> Here I find the compensation I need by imagining life as it was in days gone by
> *Prima cominciò col construire quest'ala, poi finì col rifare la casa di sana pianta*
> He started by building this wing, and he ended up by rebuilding the house from scratch

Text Notes

altrettanto
> As well as the use mentioned above, *altrettanto* also means 'the same to you':
> *Buon appetito! Grazie altrettanto* – Enjoy your meal! Thanks, the same to you.

quotidiano – daily
> *Un quotidiano* – a daily newspaper.

studioso – a scholar
> One who devotes his time to cultural and intellectual interests, as opposed to *studente* – student, one who is following a recognized course of study.

lascia stare – never mind, don't bother

il nome non ti dice nulla? – the name doesn't mean anything to you?
> Also *un piatto di cannelloni non ti dice nulla?* – what would you say to a plate of cannelloni?, *questo libro non mi dice nulla* – this book doesn't appeal to me

a me il latino non andava troppo a genio – I didn't much care for Latin

tu avevi scelto la scienza fin d'allora – even then you had already chosen science
  Scelto is the past participle of *scegliere*.

nei pressi di Formia – in the vicinity of Formia

insomma – well
  This is used before a concluding statement:
  . . . e insomma sono stato abbastanza contento di andarmene – and altogether I was
rather glad to leave, *e insomma mi sono accorto che non c'era nulla da fare* – and,
in brief, I realized that there was nothing I could do.

qualsiasi
  This adjective means 'any, any . . . at all, whatever' in affirmative sentences. It
is invariable and, like *qualche* (cf. lesson 3, page 37), it has no plural and can only
be used with nouns naming things that can be counted: *qualsiasi prestesto è buono* –
any excuse is a good one.

sono immerso fino al collo nelle attività e nelle ansietà di oggi – I'm completely in-
volved in the activities and anxieties of the present day. Note also *Sono immerso
fino al collo nel lavoro* – I'm up to my eyes in work, *sono immerso fino al collo nei
guai* – I'm up to my neck in it.

le previsioni – forecast
  le previsioni del tempo – weather forecast.

di sana pianta – from scratch, from top to bottom
  This is only said when altering something already existing in some form.

da quel pigro romano passatista che sono – as the lazy Roman that I am, always
looking to the past

Uno studioso del passato *Summary*

Dal suo amico Ezio Bertelli-Giusti, noto giornalista della capitale, Alessandro
Cossogno, il padre di Cesare, riceve una breve lezione di storia antica.
  La villa di Ezio, a Sperlonga, è al centro di una regione molto interessante dal
punto di vista storico e archeologico. Dalle finestre della villa si vedono: il monte
Circeo, già abitato centomila anni fa; i monti Ausoni, che ricordano uno degli
antichi nomi dell'Italia, Ausonia; il porto di Terracina, da dove il famoso vino
Cecubo partiva per Roma. Non si vede la città di Formia, perchè è al di là del
promontorio di Gaeta, ma va ricordato che ci passò le vacanze e ci morì il grande
uomo politico e oratore latino Cicerone.
  Nelle memorie del passato Ezio trova rifugio dalle preoccupazioni del presente,
e sufficiente serenità per affrontare il futuro.

15　La Sicilia

Tindari, rovine della città greca

Over the centuries Sicily and its inhabitants, were subjected to a series of foreign
invasions or dominations – Greek, Roman, Arab, Norman, Swabian, Angevin,
Spanish – which have not only influenced the island's culture, but probably the
character of the people. Be that as it may, the tourist who visits Sicily today may
be somewhat surprised to find that Sicilians are more reserved, less ebullient
than some of their compatriots of the mainland of Italy. They live in the largest
island in the Mediterranean, an island of great natural beauty and historical

interest, with a climate whose winters are normally mild, especially on the coast, and where the summer heat is tempered by the proximity of the sea. The coastline is long and varied; some of the resorts are large, modern and equipped with lidos, others small, modest and less frequented. The north coast is broken by numerous picturesque bays and headlands, giving many excellent harbours and small fishing ports. The south coast, on the other hand, is steep and runs in an almost straight line from north-west to south-east, with practically no natural harbours or promontories. As might be expected, the principal towns of Sicily have always been coast towns.

The island is actually a detached fragment of the great Apennine range and the north-eastern part in particular is mountainous, the highest peak being that of the volcano Mount Etna. A good road runs from Catania, on the coast, up Etna to the ski-lift which takes the tourist up to just below the crater. The facilities for winter sports are good and, if bathing in the warm waters of the Mediterranean palls, the enterprising holidaymaker can be skiing in just over an hour's ride from the coast.

Etna is not the only volcano in the area though. Off the north coast of Sicily is an archipelago of seven islands known as the Aeolian Isles, and here two more volcanoes are to be found: Vulcano, which is really only an extinct crater, and Stromboli which is still in constant eruption. Tourist facilities in the Aeolian Isles, particularly on the island of Lipari, are being rapidly improved; they can be reached either by boat from Milazzo or Messina, directly from Naples with a weekly or twice-weekly service and by hydrofoil in the summer months from Taormina, Messina or Palermo.

To anyone interested in architecture the attractions of Sicily are tremendous. There are Doric temples, some of which date from as early as the 8th century B C; there are mosaics of the 11th and 12th centuries of extraordinary beauty, and a diversity of Norman, Arabic and Byzantine architecture of great splendour and often excellent preservation. The Greek remains are concentrated largely in or near the towns of Palermo, Syracuse, Agrigento, Taormina and Catania, but one of the most attractive of the smaller centres is that of Tindari, on the north coast of the island not far from Milazzo. Here excavations are still going on and some very fine mosaic pavements have been found. The Greek city of Tyndaris was founded by Dionysius I in 396 B C and stood on a rocky promontory looking out towards the Aeolian Isles and the peninsula of Milazzo. The excavations are overshadowed on one side by the great church of the Madonna Nera, but the southern part of the wall of the original Greek city is well preserved, with its square towers and main gate. The remains of the theatre of twenty-seven tiers of seats faces the sea, with a dazzling view through old arches flanked by great umbrella pines. There is also a large building with many columns and round arches which is believed to have been the gymnasium mentioned by Cicero, who spoke of Tindari as 'a noble city'. At one time it was indeed quite large and important, before it was partly destroyed by an earthquake. The main street, which has been excavated led to the centre of the town, but now stops on the edge of the precipitous cliff.

Sicily can also offer many interesting theatrical and artistic festivals: a season of grand opera at Palermo and Catania in the spring: in the summer 'Son et Lumière' at the Greek theatre of Taormina, an international film festival at Messina and

Taormina, classical plays at Syracuse, open air opera and plays at Palermo, Enna, Trapani and Messina. And even in what we would consider the depth of winter, but which the Sicilians think of as the beginning of spring, there are traditional events such as the delightfully named Almond Blossom Festival at Agrigento in February.

Panorama delle isole

L'infermiera capo dell'officina, Marisa Garelli, è ospite in Sicilia di una sua compagna di corso, Irma Melillo, che lavora all'ospedale di Messina. Oggi le due ragazze hanno intenzione di visitare le rovine di Tindari, sulla costa tirrenica. Se la meta è bella, il viaggio per arrivarci lo è ancora di più. Irma ha scelto la strada montana che da Via Garibaldi sale verso il Colle San Rizzo e poi scende sull'altro versante. Dalla cima si gode uno stupendo panorama sulle isole Eolie.

(*From the Colle San Rizzo.*)

IRMA C'è un po' di foschia, altrimenti le vedresti tutte e sette chiaramente.

MARISA Mi sembra di vedere il fumo di Stromboli . . .

I. No, quella più vicina è Vulcano; poi c'è Lipari; Salina è nascosta dietro e oggi si vede male. Stromboli è l'ultima a sinistra.

M. E le altre due?

I. Alicudi e Filicudi le vedremo forse da Tindari. Ci rimettiamo in marcia?

M. D'accordo. Qual'è la prossima tappa?

I. Milazzo. Faremo il bagno, e poi andremo a mangiare.

*   *   *

(*Milazzo. A local guide approaches the two girls*)

CICERONE Signorine belle, volete visitare il castello?

I No grazie.

C. Ma è un castello importante assai! Garibaldi ci fu nel 1860, quando sconfisse l'esercito napoletano.

M. Se c'è già stato lui, non è il caso che ci andiamo anche noi.

C. Ma è molto antico! Fu costruito nel Duecento.

I. E noi siamo molto moderne, e vogliamo andare a pranzo.

C. Andiamo da Turiddu. È un ristorante molto buono, non troppo caro. Ieri ci venni con due americani . . .

I. Molte grazie, ma sappiamo già dove andare.

C. Se è così . . . buongiorno a voi.

M. Meno male che ci siamo liberate di questo cicerone.

I. Poveretto! in fondo non è stato troppo insistente. Chissà come ci rimarrebbe se sapesse che andiamo a mangiare proprio al ristorante dove voleva portarci lui!

*   *   *

(*Later, at Tindari*)

M. Se fotografi le isole attraverso quest'arco hai un'inquadratura magnifica. Quante pose ti restano?

I. Quattro o cinque.

M: Lasciane almeno due per i mosaici. Non hai un altro caricatore?

I. No, ma questo mi basterà. Per fortuna Tindari non è molto grande.

M. Oggi no, ma prima era molto più grande. La strada dov'eravamo pochi minuti fa, quella che s'interrompe all'orlo del precipizio, conduceva una volta al centro di Tindari.

I. Fu distrutta da un terremoto?

M. Sì, da un terremoto che fece crollare in mare metà di questa collina, insieme alla parte più importante della città e ai suoi abitanti. Dopo una simile catastrofe non ci rimase più nessuno, e anche gli edifici che si salvarono caddero in rovina.

I. Gli scavi, però, non sono ancora finiti.

M. Si può dire che siano appena cominciati, e stanno dando ottimi risultati. Vieni, voglio farti vedere i mosaici: ci sono un cervo rampante e un toro che sono davvero sorprendenti.

Language Practice

1 Pattern sentence

L'infermiera capo dell'officina, Marisa Garelli, è ospite in Sicilia di una sua compagna di corso, Irma Melillo, che lavora all'ospedale di Messina.

2 Dalla cima si gode uno stupendo panorama su tutte le isole.

Dal promontorio . . .
. . . tutte e tre . . .
. . . i castelli.
. . . vista . . .

3 Le isole sono vicine?   No, non credo che siano vicine.

Si vede Salina?
Irma va già a mangiare?
Fanno il bagno adesso?
Piero viene con noi?
La strada conduce a Tindari?
Tindari è molto grande?
Giorgio ha una sorella?
Lavorano a Milano?
Visitano oggi il castello?
Vanno al cinema?

4 Hai dato il libro a Giorgio?   Sì, gliel' ho dato.

La guida ha fatto vedere alle ragazze il castello?
Scriviamo questa cartolina ai nonni?
Hai fatto venire l'infermiera?
Hai fatto arrivare le fotografie?
Ci hai fatto mettere su la tenda?

Notes

Past Historic of verbs in *-ere*

In the past historic of most verbs in *-ere* the 2nd person singular and the 1st and 2nd person plural are formed (as for *-are* and *-ire* verbs) by replacing the infinitive endings with the following:

	VEDERE	PRENDERE
. . . .	. . . .	. . . .
-esti	vedesti	prendesti
. . . .	. . . .	. . . .
-emmo	vedemmo	prendemmo
-este	vedeste	prendeste
. . . .	. . . .	. . . .

The 1st person singular, however, has no connection with the infinitive, although in many cases it is related to the past participle; it must therefore be learnt separately, and the 3rd person singular and plural are formed from it by replacing its final *-i* with the endings *-e* and *-ero* respectively.

The complete conjugation of the past historic of the two model verbs above is therefore:

VEDERE	PRENDERE (past part. preso)
vidi	presi
vedesti	prendesti
vide	prese
vedemmo	prendemmo
vedeste	prendeste
videro	presero

In the 1st person singular and in the forms derived from it (i.e. 3rd person singular and plural), the stress always falls on the same syllable; in the forms derived from the infinitive, the stress always falls on the last syllable but one.

Of the verbs in *-are* and *-ire*, *fare*, *venire* and *dire* conform to the pattern for *-ere* verbs:

FARE	VENIRE	DIRE
feci	venni	dissi
facesti	venisti	dicesti
fece	venne	disse
facemmo	venimmo	dicemmo
faceste	veniste	diceste
fecero	vennero	dissero

Past Historic of *essere* and *avere*

ESSERE	AVERE
fui	ebbi
fosti	avesti
fu	ebbe
fummo	avemmo
foste	aveste
furono	ebbero

Text Notes

l'infermiera capo (also *la capo infermiera*) – matron, sister

Capo – head, is frequently found in compound nouns. It is normally the first element of the compound in masculine nouns. Some of these form their plural in *capi-*:

capobanda	pl. *capibanda*	bandmaster (or ringleader)
capocaccia	*capicaccia*	master of the hunt
capostazione	*capistazione*	stationmaster
capotreno	*capitreno*	guard
capolinea	*capilinea*	terminus (of a bus, tram etc.)

Other compound nouns, however, form their plural by altering the second element:

capolavoro	*capolavori*	masterpiece
capoluogo	*capoluoghi*	provincial capital

se la meta è bella, il viaggio lo è ancora di più – the destination may be beautiful, but the way there is even more beautiful

After the verb *essere*, the adjective need not be repeated, and in that case it must be replaced by the particle *lo* (cf. lesson 14, page 122).

tutte e sette – all seven of them

When *tutto* is followed by a number, *e* must precede the number: *tutti e due* both of them, *tutti e cinque* – all five of them. When *tutto* is followed by a noun, the definite article must precede the noun: *tutte le case* – all the houses, *tutta la Sicilia* – the whole of Sicily.

signorine belle . . . importante assai

The normal position of the adjective and the adverb (*belle signorine . . . assai importante*) is often reversed in the South of Italy for emphasis.

sconfisse

This is the past historic of *sconfiggere* – to defeat, past part. *sconfitto*.

se c'è già stato lui, non è il caso che ci andiamo anche noi – if he has already been there, why should we bother?

For *non è il caso*, cf. lesson 6, page 63.

Turiddu

This is a pet name deriving from *Salvaturi*, the Sicilian dialect form of *Salvatore*.

ieri ci venni

In Sicily and in other southern regions the past historic is often used where the perfect would be found more appropriate in other parts of Italy.

cicerone

The name of the Roman senator (cf. lesson 14, page 120) is familiarly given to tourist guides, often remarkable for their untiring eloquence.

in fondo – on the whole

chissà come ci rimarrebbe se sapesse che andiamo a mangiare proprio al ristorante dove voleva portarci lui – imagine how disappointed he would be if he knew that we were going to eat in the very restaurant he wanted to take us to

  Rimanerci is a shortened form of *rimanere male* – to be disappointed, *rimanere sorpreso* or *di stucco* – to be surprised.

posa – exposure (in a roll of film)

per fortuna – luckily

distrutta
  This is the past part. of *distruggere* – to destroy, past hist. *distrussi*.

una simile catastrofe – such a disaster

rimase
  This is the past historic of *rimanere* – to remain, past part. *rimasto*

caddero
  This is the past historic of *cadere* – to fall, past part. *caduto*.

Glossary

1 The meaning of the words in this glossary is usually the one they have in the context in which they appear, irrespective of any other meaning they may have in a different context.

2 Nouns and adjectives are given in their singular form. It should be assumed that nouns ending in -o are masculine and nouns ending in -a are feminine. In the case of exceptions and for all other nouns the gender and number are indicated by a definite or indefinite article. Words marked with an asterisk can be either masculine or feminine.

3 With the exception of impersonal verbs in the 3rd person, verbs are given in the infinitive, followed by the past participle in cases where it is not formed from the infinitive. The auxiliary is indicated whenever it does not conform to the rule given in lesson 2.

abbassare   *to lower*
* abitante   *inhabitant*
accalappiare   *to catch, trap*
accendere (p.p. acceso)   *to light*
accettare   *to accept*
d' accordo   *agreed, granted*
acqua dolce   *fresh water*
acquaio   *(kitchen) sink*
acquistare   *to buy; acquire*
adatto (a)   *suitable (for)*
addormentarsi   *to fall asleep*
adesso   *now*
gli affari   *business*
affatto (non . . .)   *not . . . at all*
affidare   *to entrust*
affitto   *rent*
affitto (prendere in . . .)   *to rent*
affollato   *crowded*
aggiustare   *to put right*
agosto   *August*
agricolo   *agricultural*
un agricoltore   *farmer*
aiutare   *to help*
ala   *wing*
albergo   *hotel*
albero   *tree*
allenato   *fit*
almeno   *at least*
alto   *high*
in alto   *high up*
altrettanto . . . quanto   *as . . . as, as much . . . as*

altrimenti   *otherwise*
altro   *other*
altrove   *elsewhere*
alzarsi   *to get up*
amaro   *bitter*
ammazzare   *to kill*
anfibio   *amphibious*
angolo   *corner*
annata   *year*
ansietà   *anxiety*
anticamera   *entrance hall*
di anticipo   *in advance*
antico   *ancient*
gli antichi   *people of ancient times*
anzi   *in fact*
aperitivo   *apéritif*
appena   *hardly*
approfittare di   *to take advantage of*
approfondito   *profound*
appuntamento (dare . . . a)   *to arrange to meet*
appunto   *precisely, that's it*
aprire (p.p. aperto)   *to open*
arco   *arch, archway*
arredamento   *furnishing and decoration*
arretrato   *outstanding*
l' artrite (f.)   *arthritis*
ascoltare   *to listen to*
aspettare   *to wait for*
assaggiare   *to taste*

assenza *absence*

assolutamente *absolutely, at all costs*

assumere (p.p. assunto) *to take on*

attendere (p.p. atteso) *to wait for*

attento *careful*

attimo *moment*

attirare *to attract*

attivo *active*

attrezzare *to equip*

un' automobile *car*

avvertire *to warn; advise*

avvicinarsi *to approach*

azienda *firm*

azienda agricola *farm*

bagaglio *luggage*

bagno *bathroom; bath; swim*

banco *counter*

barca *(rowing-) boat*

basso *low*

basta *it's enough*

battello *boat*

il benessere *well-being*

bere (p.p. bevuto) *to drink*

un bicchiere *glass*

biglietto *ticket*

binario *rails (platform)*

bisogna *it's necessary*

bisogno *need*

un bocchettone dell'olio *oil-filler pipe (car)*

borsa *bag*

una botte *barrel, cask*

bottiglia *bottle*

un bottone *button*

brutto *unpleasant*

buio *dark, darkness*

cadere (p.p. caduto) *to fall*

un caffè *coffee; coffee-bar*

calze *socks; stockings*

cambiare *to change*

cambio (dare il cambio a qualcuno) *to relieve someone*

camera *room*

camera da letto *bedroom*

camicia *shirt*

camionetta *van*

camoscio *chamois*

campagnolo *countryman*

campeggiare *to camp*

campeggio *camping*

cancello *gate*

capace *capable*

capire *to understand*

una capitale *capital*

capitare *to happen*

capo *head*

cappella *chapel*

un carattere *character*

un caricatore *spool*

cartolina *postcard*

caso *case*

cassa *cash desk*

castelli in aria *castles in Spain*

cattivo *bad*

cedere (p.p. ceduto) *to give, release*

cedro *cedar-tree*

cena, cenetta *supper*

cercare *to try; look for*

cerino *wax match*

certo *certainly*

cervo *deer*

cestino *picnic meal; small basket*

chiacchierare *to chat*

chiamare *to call*

chiamarsi *to be called*

chiaramente *clearly*

una chiave *key*

chiedere (p.p. chiesto) *to ask*

chiesa *church*

chilo *kilo (2·205 lbs.)*

chilometro *kilometre (1093·63 yards)*

chissà *who knows*

chiudere (p.p. chiuso) *to close*

un cicerone *tourist guide*

cima *summit*

cioè *that is*

circa *about*
cognato *brother-in-law*
coincidenza *connection (train etc.)*
un colle, una collina *hill*
collo *neck*
a colori *in colour*
cominciare (a) *to begin*
comitiva *party*
* commerciante *trader, merchant*
un commerciante ortofrutticolo *market gardener*
commercio *trade*
commessa *salesgirl*
comodamente *comfortably*
compenso *compensation*
complesso *ensemble*
comprare *to buy*
comprendere (p.p. compreso) *to include*
compromesso *compromise*
comunque *anyway*
condurre (p.p. condotto) *to take; lead*
connettere (p.p. connesso) *to connect*
conoscenza *knowledge*
conoscenza (fare la . . . di) *to make the acquaintance of*
conoscere (p.p. conosciuto) *to know*
conserva (mettere in . . .) *to pickle, preserve (food)*
consiglio *piece of advice*
contabilità *accountancy*
contare *to count*
un contatore *meter*
contiguo *adjoining*
contributo *contribution*
conversare *to converse*
conviene *it's better*
coppa dell'olio *oil sump*
coprire (p.p. coperto) *to cover*
correre (p.p. corso) *to run*
correre in macchina *to travel (of a car)*
corridoio *corridor*

corso *course*
così . . . come *as . . . as*
costa *coast*
costeggiare *to keep to the coast*
costruire *to build*
crema solare *sun lotion*
cresta *ridge*
criticare *to criticize*
crollare *to collapse*
cucina *cookery, cooking; kitchen*
cucinare *to cook*
cucire *to sew*
cugino, -a *cousin*
cultura *culture*
cuocere (p.p. cotto) *to cook (the process of cooking)*
cuoio *leather*
cura *cure; care*
cura dimagrante *slimming cure*

dappertutto *everywhere*
dattilografa *typist*
davanti (a) *in front of*
davvero *indeed, really*
decidere (p.p. deciso) *to decide*
deludere (p.p. deluso) *to disillusion*
desiderare *to wish*
dietro (a) *behind*
un dilemma *dilemma*
dilettevole *pleasurable*
dimenticare *to forget*
i dintorni *surrounding districts*
* dipendente *employee*
dire (p.p. detto) *to say*
un direttore *director, manager*
dirigere (p.p. diretto) *to manage*
diritto *straight*
disappunto *disappointment*
disastro *disaster*
un disegnatore *draughtsman*
disfare (p.p. disfatto) *to unpack*
distrarre (p.p. distratto) *to distract*
distratto *absent-minded*

distruggere (p.p. distrutto) *to destroy*
ditta *firm*
diventare *to become*
diverso *different; several*
divertimento *amusement*
divertirsi *to enjoy oneself*
dividere (p.p. diviso) *to share*
divorare *to devour*
doccia *shower*
dopotutto *after all*
dormire (aux. avere) *to sleep*
un dottore *doctor (University graduate)*
dovere (p.p. dovuto) *to have to*

eccellente *excellent*
eccezionale *exceptional*
edificio *building*
elettrodomestico *electric house-hold appliance*
equilibrio *balance*
ad esempio *for instance*
un esemplare *specimen*
esercito *army*
esistere (p.p. esistito) *to exist*
un' estate *summer*
estendere (p.p. esteso) *to stretch*
un' estensione *extension*
esterno *external*
l' estero *abroad*
estivo (adj.) *summer*
ettaro *hectare (2·471 acres)*

fabbrica *factory*
facile *easy*
faggeta *beech-wood*
fama *reputation*
un fannullone *idler, lazibones*
fantasia *imagination; flight of fancy*
fantasticare *to indulge in flights of fancy, day-dream*
fastidio *annoyance*
fatto *fact*

favola *tale*
ferie *holidays*
fermarsi *to stop*
fetta *slice*
a fianco *beside*
fidanzato, -a *fiancé, fiancée*
fiducia *trust*
figurarsi *to imagine*
finchè *as long as*
fin d'allora *since then*
un fiume *river*
un fondatore *founder*
una fondazione *foundation*
in fondo *after all, on the whole*
fontana *spring, fountain*
forare *to puncture*
forse *perhaps*
forte *large; strong*
foschia *haze*
fra (tra) *within, in; between, among*
il francese *French language*
francobollo *postage stamp*
fratello maggiore *elder brother*
fresco *cool*
in fretta *quickly*
frigorifero *refrigerator*
di fronte *opposite*
fuga *escape*
fumo *smoke*
funzionare *to function*
fuori *outside*
una fuoriserie *a special model*
furgoncino *van*

gamba *leg*
un generale *general (army)*
un genere *kind*
un gestore *manager (shop)*
giallo *yellow*
un giornale *daily newspaper*
giornata *day, working day*
giovane *young*
girare *to turn*
in giro *around*
gita *outing, trip*
giù *down (south)*

giudicare *to judge*
giugno *June*
giusto *precisely; right*
godere (p.p. goduto) *to enjoy*
golfo *gulf*
gomma *car tyre*
gradimento *liking*
grano *wheat*
grave *serious*
grazioso *pretty*
gridare *to shout*
grosso *big*
grotta *grotto*
grugnito *grunt*
guardare *to look at*
guardarsi da *to beware of*
guardia *keeper*
guastare *to wreck*
guida *guide*
guidare *to drive*
gusto *taste*

ieri *yesterday*
imbarazzo *embarrassment*
imbarcare *to ship*
immergere (p.p. immerso) *to immerse*
immischiarsi *to meddle*
impalcatura *scaffolding*
un imperatore *emperor*
impiastro *nuisance*
impiego *employment, job*
importare *to matter*
incontrare *to meet, come across*
infermiera *nurse*
infilare *to slip on*
un ingegnere *engineer*
Inghilterra *England*
inglese *English*
ingordo *greedy*
ingresso *entrance*
inquadratura *frame*
insieme *together*
insomma *in short*
intatto *intact*
intellettuale *intellectual*

intendere (p.p. inteso) *to intend, mean to*
intercambiabile *interchangeable*
interno *inside*
* interprete *interpreter*
interrompere (p.p. interrotto) *to stop*
intorno (a) *around*
invece *instead; on the other hand*
invitato *guest*
isola *island*

lago *lake*
lamentarsi *to grumble*
lampadina *(electric) bulb*
lampo elettronico *flash (photographic)*
lasciare *to leave; allow*
lavatoio *washroom*
una lavatrice *washing-machine*
letto *bed*
lì *there*
libero *free*
un limone *lemon, lemon tree*
luccicare *to glitter*
la luce *light; electricity*
luglio *July*
a lungo *for a long time*
luogo *place*

macchina *car*
macchina da cucire *sewing machine*
magari *perhaps; even*
un magazziniere *storekeeper*
magazzino (grande ...) *department store*
un maglione *sweater*
magro *slim, thin*
mandare *to send*
mandorla *almond*
mandorlo *almond-tree*
una manifestazione *spectacle*
in marcia *on one's way*
massaia *housewife*
masseria *farm*
materia *material things*

meccanico *mechanic*
meglio *better*
mensa *canteen*
una mente *mind*
mentre *while*
mercato *market*
un mese *month*
metà *half*
meta *destination*
metterci *to take (time)*
mettere (p.p. messo) *to put*
mezzo di trasporto *means of transport*
mezzogiorno *noon*
mezz'ora *half an hour*
mica (non . . .) *not . . . at all; not . . . possibly*
minestra *soup*
modello *model*
una moglie *wife*
montagna *mountain*
mosaico *mosaic*
mostra *exhibition; show*
un motore *engine*
muovere (p.p. mosso) *to move*
musica da camera *chamber music*

nascondere (p.p. nascosto) *to hide*
natio *native*
nè . . . nè *neither . . . nor*
negozio *shop*
nemmeno *not even*
nero *black*
nessuno *no one*
niente *nothing*
* nipote *nephew, niece*
noioso *boring*
noleggiare *to hire*
nonno, -a, -i *grandfather, grandmother, grandparents*
noto *well-known*
una notte *night*
nuora *daughter-in-law*
nuotata *swim*
nuovo *new*

obbiettivo *lens*
un' occasione *opportunity*
occhiata (dare un' . . .) *to glance*
occorre *it is necessary*
l' occorrente (m.) *what is necessary*
occuparsi *to attend to; take an interest in*
officina *workshop; factory*
olio *oil*
oliva *olive*
olivo *olive-tree*
oltre *beyond*
ombra *shade*
ombroso *shaded*
opera *opera; work*
ora *hour; now*
orlo *edge*
ormai *by now*
ornare *to adorn*
orso *bear; grumpy person*
ortofrutticolo (adj.) *fruit and vegetable*
un ospedale *hospital*
* ospite *guest*
ottimo *very good*

pacchetto *packet*
un paese *village*
paesino *small village*
palazzo comunale *town hall*
il pane *bread*
pantaloni *trousers*
pare (p.p. parso) *it seems*
partire *to leave*
partire (a . . . da) *from*
Pasqua *Easter*
* passatista *nostalgic person*
passato *past*
un passavivande *service hatch*
passeggero *passenger*
passeggiare (aux. avere) *to stroll*
passo *step; pass; pace*
paura (avere . . .) *to be afraid*
una pendice *hillside*

137

pensare *to think of*
pensiero (essere in . . .) *to be anxious*
una pensione *boarding-house*
pentola *saucepan*
per *for ; through*
perciò *therefore*
percorrere (p.p. percorso) *to travel over*
perdere (p.p. perso, perduto) *to lose*
permesso *permit*
permettere (p.p. permesso) *to allow*
di persona *in person*
pesante *heavy*
la pesca subacquea *underwater fishing*
un pesce *fish*
piacere (p.p. piaciuto) *to be pleasing*
il piacere *pleasure*
piano *plan ; floor*
pianta (di sana . . .) *from scratch*
piantare *to set up*
pianura *plain*
piazzare *to sell on the market*
un piede *foot*
pienamente *fully*
pieno *full*
pigliare *to catch*
pigro *lazy*
pineta *pine-wood*
pino *pine-tree*
pioggia *rain*
pittoresco *picturesque*
piuttosto *rather*
un po' *a little*
un polpettone *meat-loaf*
poltrona *arm-chair*
un pontile *pier, landing stage*
porcheria *rubbish*
porta d'ingresso *entrance door*
portafoglio *wallet*
portare (qualcuno) *to bring (someone)*
portico *portico*

un portiere *gate keeper*
porto *port*
posa *exposure*
possedere (p.p. posseduto) *to have, own*
posteriore *rear*
posticino *nice spot*
posto *place*
pranzo *lunch*
praticare *to practise, pursue*
precipizio *cliff, precipice*
preciso *precise, definite*
preferire *to prefer*
prego *please*
prendere (p.p. preso) *to take*
prenotare *to book*
preoccuparsi *to worry*
una preoccupazione *worry*
presentare *to introduce*
i pressi *surroundings*
prestare *to lend*
prestito (chiedere in . . .) *to borrow*
pretesto *pretext*
una previsione *forecast*
prezzo di costo *cost price*
prima (di) *before*
un problema *problem*
prodotto *produce*
produrre (p.p. prodotto) *to produce*
un programma *plan, programme*
promettere (p.p. promesso) *to promise*
promontorio *promontory*
pronto *ready*
proporre (p.p. proposto) *to propose*
a proposito *by the way*
proprietario, -a *owner*
proprio *just, really*
prosa *prose, drama*
proseguire *to continue*
prospero *prosperous*
prossimo *coming, next*
un pullman *coach (bus)*
punto *point*

qua *here*
quadrato *square*
qualche *some*
qualcuno *somebody, someone*
quanto *how long*
quarto *quarter*
quasi *almost, nearly*
quassù *up here*
qui *here*
quindi *therefore*
quindicina *about fifteen; fortnight*
un quintale *quintal (about 2 cwt)*
quotidiano *daily*

raccolto *harvest*
raccontare *to tell*
raggio *radius*
raggiungere (p.p. raggiunto) *to reach*
una ragione *reason*
ragione (avere . . .) *to be right*
rampante *rampant*
rapido *express train*
razza *sort*
realizzare *to realize, make something come true*
recarsi *to go*
una regione *region*
remare *to row*
remata *spell at the oars*
reparto *department*
resa *yield*
restare *to stay, remain*
restaurare *to restore*
resto *change*
retta (dare . . . a) *to pay attention to*
riavere (p.p. riavuto) *to have back*
di ricambio *spare*
ricco *rich*
ricevere (p.p. ricevuto) *to receive*
ricevimento *party, reception*
ricoprire (p.p. ricoperto) *to cover completely*

ricordare *to remind, remember*
ridurre (p.p. ridotto) *to reduce*
riempire *to fill*
rifare (p.p. rifatto) *to rebuild*
rimanere (p.p. rimasto) *to remain, stay*
rimettersi in marcia *to resume one's journey*
rimodernare *to modernize*
rimorchiare *to tow*
rimorchio (tirare a . . .) *to tow*
rinfrescare *to freshen up*
riparare *to repair*
ripararsi *to shelter*
ripetere (p.p. ripetuto) *to repeat*
a riposo *retired*
ripostiglio *box room*
risolvere (p.p. risolto) *to solve*
risparmiare *to save*
risparmio *saving*
rispondere (p.p. risposto) *to reply, answer*
ritirata *withdrawal*
ritornare *to return*
riuscire *to succeed*
roba *stuff*
rovina *ruin*
in rovina *in ruins*
rubinetto *tap*
un rumore *noise*
ruota *wheel*

sabato *Saturday*
sala da pranzo *dining-room*
salato *salted*
il sale *salt*
salire *to go up, climb*
saltare fuori *to come out in the open*
salutare *to greet, say 'hello'*
salvarsi *to escape; survive*
sapere (p.p. saputo) *to know (how to)*
sasso *stone; rock*
sbagliare *to make a mistake*
sbrigare *to get through*

scaldabagno   *water-heater*
scambiare   *to mistake*
scarpa   *shoe*
scatoletta   *small box*
scavo   *excavation*
scegliere (p.p. scelto)   *to choose*
scendere (p.p. sceso)   *to go down; get out (of a train)*
sciacquìo   *noise of water lapping*
sciare   *to ski*
scienza   *science*
sciocchezza   *silly statement, nonsense*
sciocco   *silly*
scommettere (p.p. scommesso)   *to bet*
scompartimento   *compartment*
sconfiggere (p.p. sconfitto)   *to defeat*
sconto   *discount*
scoprire (p.p. scoperto)   *to discover; uncover*
scrivere (p.p. scritto)   *to write*
scuotere (p.p. scosso)   *to shake*
scusarsi   *to excuse oneself*
sedentario   *sedentary*
sedere (p.p. seduto)   *to sit*
un sedile   *seat*
segreto   *secret*
sembrare   *to seem*
semisdraiato   *reclining*
semplice   *simple*
sempre   *always*
sentire   *to listen*
serata   *evening*
servirsi di   *to use*
sfogliare   *to leaf through*
sicario   *hired killer*
siccità   *drought*
siccome   *as, since*
sicuro   *sure*
silenzioso   *silent, quiet*
sistemare   *to arrange*
snello   *slim*
soddisfare (p.p. soddisfatto)   *to satisfy*
la soddisfazione   *satisfaction*

soggiorno   *living-room*
solamente   *only*
* solista   *soloist*
solito   *usual*
solito (come al . . .)   *as usual*
sonnecchiare   *to doze*
sorella maggiore   *elder sister*
una sorgente   *spring, source*
sorprendente   *surprising*
sosta   *stop*
sotto   *under(neath)*
una specie   *species*
la spedizione   *dispatch*
spegnere (p.p. spento)   *to put out*
sperare   *to hope*
sperimentale   *experimental*
spesa   *cost, outlay*
spesso   *often*
spia   *pilot-light*
spiaggia   *seashore*
spiegare   *to explain*
spingersi (p.p. spinto)   *to go as far as*
spirito   *spirit*
spiritoso   *funny*
sporgersi (p.p. sporto)   *to lean out*
sportello   *hatch*
sposarsi   *to get married*
staccarsi   *to detach oneself*
stanco   *tired*
stanza   *room*
una stazione   *railway station*
stesso   *same*
storia   *history*
strada   *road*
straniero   *foreigner*
strategico   *strategic*
stretto   *narrow*
striscia   *strip*
studio   *study*
stupendo   *stupendous*
su!   *come on!*
subito   *at once*
succedere (p.p. successo)   *to happen*

svelto   *quick*
sviluppare   *to develop*

tabaccheria   *tobacconist's shop*
tagliare   *to cut*
tappa   *stage; stop*
tappo   *cap*
tardi (adv.)   *late*
tardo   *late*
tavola   *table*
tavolino   *small table*
tecnico   *technical; technician*
tempo   *weather; time*
a tempo   *in time*
tenda   *tent*
tenere (p.p. tenuto)   *to keep*
tentare   *to tempt*
terrazza   *terrace, sun roof*
terrazzo   *terrace*
terremoto   *earthquake*
tirare avanti   *to carry on*
tornare   *to return*
un tornitore   *machine-lathe operator*
toro   *bull*
tortuoso   *twisting*
tra, fra   *within*
tranquillo   *quiet*
trascinare   *to drag*
tratta (si . . . di)   *it's a question of*
trattenersi (p.p. trattenuto)   *to stay*
tratto   *stretch*
un treppiede   *tripod*
trovare   *to find*
trovare (andare a . . .)   *to visit*

tuffarsi   *to dive*
* turista   *tourist*
a turno   *in turn*

ufficio commerciale   *marketing department*
uguale   *same*
ultimo   *last*
unico   *only*
utile   *useful*

valico   *pass*
valigia   *suitcase*
una valle   *valley*
vedere (p.p. visto, veduto)   *to see*
ventilato   *airy*
vento   *wind*
verità   *truth*
un versante   *side, slope*
verso   *towards*
vestirsi   *to dress*
vestitino   *nice little dress*
viaggio   *journey*
viaggio di nozze   *honeymoon*
un vice-direttore   *assistant manager*
vicino (a)   *near*
villeggiatura   *holiday*
vino   *wine*
vista   *view, panorama*
vizio   *bad habit*
voglia (avere . . . di)   *to feel like*
un volante   *steering wheel*
volentieri   *willingly*
volta   *time, occasion*

zio, zia   *uncle, aunt*
zona   *zone*

Index to main grammar notes

N.B. In each case the figures refer to the lesson number

Acknowledgment is due to the following for permission to reproduce illustrations:
  CAMERA PRESS LTD St. Vitale, Ravenna (Camerafoto), page 30, Spoleto (Bernard G. Silberstein), page 40
  J. ALLAN CASH cloisters, front cover, Milan, page 10, Garda, page 20, Nuraghi, page 105
  COURTAULD INSTITUTE OF ART La Certosa di Pavia, page 57
  BLACK STAR Urbino, page 65
  ELSIE FERGUSON Tindari, page 125
  GIANNI BERENGO GARDIN Alberobello, page 82
  ITALIAN STATE TOURIST OFFICE Festa dei Ceri, page 38, chessboard, page 47, Abruzzi, page 74, Palio, Siena, page 80, Canolo, page 113, Gaeta, page 119
  A. F. KERSTING Lucca, page 98
  MONITOR PRESS FEATURES LTD Monterosso, page 89
  POPPERFOTO Padua, page 48

Published by the British Broadcasting Corporation
35 Marylebone High Street, London W1M 4AA

© The authors and the British Broadcasting Corporation 1968

First published 1968
Reprinted 1968, 1971
Printed Offset Litho in Great Britain by Cox & Wyman Limited,
London, Fakenham and Reading

SBN 563 08315 8